THE EUROPEAN NOVELISTS SERIES

*Edited by Herbert Van Thal*

# ANTHONY TROLLOPE

*Uniform with this Volume*

# ANTHONY TROLLOPE

## BEATRICE CURTIS BROWN

**ARTHUR BARKER LIMITED**
5 WINSLEY STREET LONDON W1

SBN 213 17902 4

Printed in Great Britain by
Lowe & Brydone (Printers) Ltd., London

# PREFACE

THIS book is intended as a discussion of Trollope as a novelist and deals no more than is essential with the facts of his life. For these the reader is referred to his own Autobiography and to Mr. Michael Sadleir's *Trollope : A Commentary*—a book to which every writer on Trollope must be indebted, since it covers not only every relevant detail of Trollope's life, but also includes most interesting material dealing with him from the writings or memories of his contemporaries. It is impossible in a short book, in fact, to cover both Trollope's life and works, and it is more particularly his works that call for examination and assessment to-day. Even so, I have not been able to do more than suggest a few lines of thought : it will be many years before every Trollope enthusiast will be able to feel that everything has been said that should be said about Trollope. I hope, however, I have started a few hares and have drawn attention to some of his books—and particularly some aspects of his books—which have been, I think, overlooked or underestimated.

I wish to make grateful acknowledgment for the help I have received from Sir Paul Sinker, Director General of the British Council and Mr. J. M. Newton, Director and Personnel, G.P.O., who provided me with some of the material on Trollope's opinions and career in the Civil Service contained in Chapter VIII; and in general to my late Civil Service colleagues from whom I learned to understand Trollope's own respect and devotion for that Service.

B. C. B.

## NOTE TO SECOND EDITION

At the time this book was written, the general view of the Victorian era was still biased by Lytton Strachey's iconoclasm —far less respectful or sympathetic than today. Since then there has been a spate of social histories, 19th century biographies and memoirs—headed by the famous BBC Third Programme Victorian Series of 1951. If I had been writing this Introduction today, I would have assumed (rather than made a case for) a more sympathetic attitude from the reader than I could in 1949 when the book was finished. Nevertheless, I hope that it will still provide a helpful background to Trollope's works and attitude for those who are, at least, less concerned with history than with fiction.

B.C.B. 1969

## I

THE novelist who uses contemporary life for his material has to be capable of freeing himself from the preconceptions of his age if his work is to have a lasting validity ; if he is dominated by his times he will produce only interesting period pieces—though he may redeem them by poetic power, beauty of language or technique in construction. The number of English novelists who have been able consistently to rise above topicality are few ; it is a difficult thing to do, for contemporary preoccupations include not only the conventions of the time but also the mental and social conflicts. To sift the eternal from these conflicts and conventions which colour every act and thought requires great natural artistry, great detachment or a total comprehension of life as history which is not often found with creative ability.

A great novelist may well deal with life in terms of his time, but these terms will supply the furnishings of his work rather than the substance. He will handle current ideas, prejudices and customs, but his judgment and his sensibilities will not be bounded by these and if he is successful— if to some extent he achieves greatness—the sympathy and judgment of his readers at any age will respond to his own. He and his future readers will both be talking about the same thing.

Anthony Trollope achieved greatness as a novelist in this sense and he is an interesting example of greatness in novel-writing because he appears to have no usually recognised qualities of greatness in himself and because he wrote at a time when it was, one would imagine, very difficult to detach oneself from the contemporary world ; the *moeurs* and the *mores* of the Victorian age exercised a very powerful hold upon the people of the time and nearly all writers were either subjugated by them or else reacted away from them—and reaction is as topical as submission. Trollope had, in a sense, everything against him ; not only did he lack poetic power and grandeur of language but he employed a readable unexacting style from which he could not hope to make the purely topical or the purely theatrical appear to be anything more impressive. His values, in fact, lay exposed, in very workaday clothes indeed.

What is remarkable about him is that although he was, intellectually, what passes for an " ordinary " man, and although he lived in an age of conflicts and in a society which made most restricting demands on novelists, he kept his balance and maintained his own direct view of human affairs. Above all, he did not attempt to escape from any dilemma with which the social scene presented him by confining himself to special cases—by writing, that is to say, about anomalies, or, as he might so easily have done with his talent for comedy, by making a corner in the obscure and the " quaint." On the contrary, he took, in the greater part of his books, a broad canvas, often dealing with several layers of society in his multiple plots.

Using society as it lay to hand, its manners, its attitudes, its prejudices, he constructed an immense series of dramas, nearly all of which turned upon personal relations, professional struggles or political skirmishings and, without rancour, without highlighting his own messengers among the characters and without distortion, he contrived to present a point of view which was predominantly his own.

As a result—though this may appear paradoxical—Trollope stands out in the stream of English literature as an Englishman ; as, that is to say, the concrete example of an abstraction. Throughout the generations, English readers hearing Trollope's own voice in his writings will say, " That was like my father." His writings represent an attitude of mind which we feel to be indigenous—a summing up of English quality. This quality does not belong to any period and is not moulded by any purely topical convention.

The accepted idea of a great novelist is so much at odds with the accepted idea of Trollope and his work that it takes some searching out of his work to see why he achieved validity when so many others who had gifts he did not possess failed to do so. The answer seems to be that Trollope possessed in a singular degree direct vision—or it might be less tendentious to say " a clear channel." Experience, objects seen and things heard, came straight through to his receiving set. They did not arrive distorted or mutilated or even improved by his having, as it were, advanced to meet them with his critical faculties waving ahead of him like antennae. He simply received ; judgment was passed later. His judgment was formed upon things as they were, not on what he had chosen to make them before the knowledge of them had entered into him. He could be called an automatic writer ; his creative and receptive powers were far greater than his critical powers. And though he voiced his opinions of other writers and indeed laid down the law about writing, he did not set himself up as a critic ; his criticism might be said to belong to his life rather than to his work. He was, by nature, utterly lacking in that kind of vanity which impels many writers to cut a dash as philosophers. It was this lack of vanity, possibly, which kept his channel so clear for his receptive powers. He did not muddy it with a projection of his own mentality.

It is not necessary, in order to enjoy Trollope, to know anything of the background of his time ; but such a knowledge greatly widens enjoyment of his work. In the first place, if we detect something more in him than merely the qualities of a good Victorian story-teller, we have a hankering to know where he takes an independent line from his time, and in the second place, we can, by making ourselves at least superficially familiar with social conditions of his times, partly remove a barrier which a century's changes have set up between him and ourselves. The reader of the future, being himself packed with current political, social and moral notions, cannot always comprehend the social or other pressures bearing upon a writer's characters (I emphasise the word " characters "—the writer himself may be unmoved by these topical pressures) ; he may, therefore, dismiss much that is beyond his experience as quaint, and, equally fatuously, admire much that is second-rate simply because it is recognisable to him.

To assess Trollope's claim to greatness in novel-writing (a claim which he would never have made for himself), it is, then, worth while glancing at the social world in which he moved—at those things which he must have taken for granted—so that it may be possible to distinguish both those elements of nineteenth-century life which would be likely to build up a point of view, and from which, therefore, a great novelist must assert some detachment, and the elements which might be called the furniture of the world—that is, the fashions, conventions and physical phenomena which, though they may affect action superficially, do not have, for a great novelist, any binding influence on imagination.

In the 1860s and '70s—at the time of Trollope's greatest popularity—people of middle age could remember an England which differed very little in essentials from Elizabeth's England, very little, certainly, as far as the tempo of its life was concerned. Since Waterloo, however, some interesting experiments by scientists in the north had completely changed the face of the land. From these experiments had come acres of factories housing multiple looms, miles of railways, steamships, the electric telegraph, the mass production of objects, the mass movement of people. A man on Mars, or some being whose time is only slightly more distended than our own, could have looked down and seen the surface of England visibly darkening, the railway lines running out, bifurcating, twining ; the cities increasing from dots to black, sprawling blots over the green. England would have appeared to be consumed, to have been injected with iron which spread through her veins and erupted here and there—particularly in the north.

It is too easy to exaggerate the effect of change on the people of a nation. The average citizen to-day is not shaken to the core when he turns on his wireless and he even assimilates the idea of an atomic bomb. His attitude to God or to his fellow-men has not been visibly shifted by short-wave communication ; his neuroses appear to have been known to Shakespeare. Nevertheless, and allowing for over-dramatisation, the speeding up of life by mechanisation in the nineteenth century must have had an effect that we can hardly assess. Every minute saved meant more activity to the hour, more production, more encounters with more people. Life was geared to an entirely different rhythm from that of the past and one might say that everyone lived three times as long as their parents had lived—reckoning life in terms of physical experience. This speeding up of life increased the number of possible objectives, the number of deals which could be pulled off in a given time and this in turn produced a restlessness, an ever unsatisfied ambition.

Ambition—for wealth, for power, for social elevation—consumed the nineteenth-century middle class and made them unhappy, for they rarely envisaged exactly what it was that was going to satisfy them. No abiding pleasure remained to them after they had counted up their possessions and their titles. Indeed, the very things they supposed they sought were disappearing at the very time they gained the wealth which was to procure them. The rise of the middle class had eaten away the political supremacy of the aristocracy and as this supremacy decayed, so the social prestige that accompanied it decayed. There was never again to exist that Parnassus of nobility to which the rising tradesman had aspired. The desire to acquire alternated with a sense of frustration and beneath the swing of this pendulum the personal and social ethic was shifted from its base position in national life. Men of goodwill felt uneasy and men of vision were anguished.

Society was distressed by yet another consequence of its industrial age. Large numbers of people were defunctionalised. Both those who had lost money—the aristocracy and landed gentry whose fortunes had either been spent or who found themselves worse off for the political and economic changes—and, in many cases, those who had gained money, had nothing particular to do and had nothing to *be*. Those whose tradesmen fathers had come up in the world and who had been brought up to be gentlefolk, had no niche. They did not care to work and they had not enough education to play. In an earlier age they might have thrown their money about with gusto, fought, gambled, gone a-soldiering. But all that was becoming less and less the thing to do ; besides they had hardly the energy. Or they could have collected, gone on the grand tour, financed poor writers for the prestige of a flowery dedication, built castles. But this needed culture ; it called for time to study, read and investigate—and the time which was saved in taking a train to Manchester did not allow for that ; it only allowed of taking another train to Newmarket. Time was not now an ever moving stream but a series of quick changes. The minds of the new class were conditioned to this tempo and it was inconceivable that they could have adjusted themselves to deal with matters which slowed them down and demanded prolonged concentration.

We cannot be sure how far Trollope understood the cause of this lack of function which so gravely undermined the vitality of the middle class ; he did not go in for historical analysis. But he drew the most complete picture of the operation of lack of function and of its effect in *The Way We Live Now*—a classic story of Victorian upper-class society at its worst ; while the weakening of the mental fibre of even the politically active youth can be seen if one compares, say, the engaging but half-baked young Lord Silverbridge of *The Duke's Children*, with the brilliant, outrageous young men of Fox's day, who gambled away their fortunes at Almack's till midnight, wrote Latin verses till dawn and dumbfounded the House of Commons by their oratory after dinner.

This demoralisation did not, of course, touch the great men—the great statesmen, professional men or scholars. They were indeed the exceptions which proved the rule, for they had a function, or if not a defined function then resources of the mind. It did not touch the great aristocrats whose position was now being assailed, whose strength lay not in their money but in their power, a power seriously threatened by the Reform Bills. For all their extravagance and frequent unscrupulousness, these felt themselves responsible at least for the people who lived on their lands and they carried that sense of responsibility into Parliament. " The Duke of Rutland is as selfish a man as any of his class . . . but partly from a sense of duty, partly from inclination, he devotes time and labour to the interest and welfare of the people who live and labour on his estate." Grevile wrote this in the earlier part of the century, but the tradition remained. There was, too, a set form of life for such as these ; they had the dignity of office (though it might be only a sinecure) and the pride of position to maintain, though this might mean only the spending of a great deal of money in particular ways—giving parties, keeping up houses, conspiring to put governments in or out, angling to get your protégé elected to Parliament. Nevertheless, all this provided a framework of life which was recognised as part of the English scene.

It may have been some vague awareness that the great aristocrats had this sense of function which was so vainly to be sought among the middle class as a whole, that produced a sort of shamefaced nostalgia for even the most shocking of the old aristocrats among the writers of the day. They tended, at any rate, to be obsessed with the memory of wicked dukes of a slightly earlier day ; Thackeray has his Steyne ;

Disraeli, more indulgent, dwells longingly on several large-scale but magnificent reprobates, and Trollope of course had Omnium, the prototype of all that a Duke had been and could be no more. Trollope, however, was less of a snob than the other two for he had a perfectly clear idea in his mind of the advantages of wealth and position. He was not at all ashamed of liking them and he placed them in the position that he believed they rated, relative to good food, books, leisure and so on. He was therefore able to write without uneasiness about the aristocracy and in the passage on the death of the old Duke of Omnium, in *Phineas Redux*, and again in the passage on the bestowal of the Garter, in *The Prime Minister*, he sums up the difference between the old tradition and the new as well as any historian has done.

The dominant class was, of course, the huge new middle class, a class now centred on the big cities but which had derived from a small town or a country background, or from a society as circumscribed and unambitious as a small town society even though it resided in London. It sprang from a level hitherto socially unrecognised and it was now called on to adapt itself to a life for which its members had, in many cases, neither the intellectual resources nor the accepted social attributes. The people from whom they sprang had been and remained the backbone of England ; upright, serious, kindly, courageous in the face of difficulties, intelligent about their work and proud of it. They were, as they remained, inclined to snobbery—frightened and overwhelmed by a title—given to talking and thinking in slogans, evasive of thought, insular, intolerant of foreigners or of those below them socially. If a member of this now ascendant class possessed adaptibility, thoughtfulness and imagination, if he inherently possessed or acquired a love of learning and a sense of curiosity, then he could rise head and shoulders above the general level of his countrymen. The greatest men of the time came from this new middle class—Peel, Cobden, Bright, Gladstone among them—and a host of thinkers, writers and scientists. But most contented themselves with wealth and carried into their new life their old parochialisms, snobberies and suspicions of " the different."

A good deal has been said in our time about Victorian prudery and hypocrisy. When condemning these unpleasant qualities we should, perhaps, remember that the Victorians had known, or their parents had known the laxity of the earlier age, a laxity which could lead to a sort of brutal cynicism which elbowed out delicacy and tenderness. We might also remember that London—at least the polite part of it—had till recently been the abode of the aristocracy, a small society representing to the outer world rather what Hollywood represents to-day : glamour and extravagance. How " they " behaved in London was not personally important to the sober burghers of the country towns or the suburbs. But when the middle class itself became metropolitan, it was necessary that a new " normal " manner of living should be imposed. To let down the barriers to the extent that had been tolerated by the aristocracy would have led to chaos ; besides the unsophisticated women of the new class could never have endured it—they were not hardened to such play upon their emotions.

There was, of course, no conscious train of thought of this kind among the Victorians when they set up their white tents of purity. The immediate causes of the growth of " Victorian morality " can be found in any social history book. The new sect of Methodism which took so strong a hold upon the artisans and lower middle class in the eighteenth century was largely responsible, as well as the reaction of the monarch and the court from the gay days of George IV ; a still greater part in building up the prevailing religious temper of the time was played by the horror of the French Revolution—which appeared as atheism in action. These were the immediate causes. But the deep hold which the narrow sexual code had on the English people at this time could scarcely be accounted for by any temporary or topical impulse ; it had its roots in a reasonable sense of social security.

This code was, of course, also a rather proud banner waved at the retreating upper classes by those who were pushing at them from below : " We may not be elegant, but we are pure ! " Bagehot wrote in 1867, " The aristocracy live in fear of the middle classes—of the grocer and the merchant. They dare not frame a society of enjoyment as the French aristocracy once framed it."

Necessarily, at least to our eyes, they went too far. The pattern of behaviour possible for a young woman, and for a young man confronted with a young woman, was set within such narrow limits—so little freedom of motion was allowed in the dance (metaphorically speaking)—that it is difficult for us to believe that feeling itself was not atrophied by lack of exercise. But it is probably a mistake for us to pity the heroines of the time for their lack of freedom (as we somewhat tendentiously phrase it) or to suppose that they were necessarily less emotionally sophisticated than ourselves. Trollope's high-spirited young women, his Violet Effinghams, Mary Lowthers, Mabel Grexes, his beloved Lady Glencora, are as ironic, as passionate, as adventurous in spirit as any women have ever been ; they

A.T.—2

did not resent their shackles any more consciously than we resent the social restrictions of our own day ; and Trollope (as we know from his professional career) was not one to endure, or to allow others to endure, unreasonable restrictions on personal liberty. Certainly, the distance allowed between the proper and the improper seems to us to be cruelly short. The enchanting Lady Glencora approached sin simply by waltzing too boisterously with Burgo Fitzgerald and we, reading of it now, rebel against the judgment passed on her (for it is clear that the waltz itself was reprehensible apart from the understanding between the partners). But in fact she herself recognised, though she resented, this judgment ; it is we, not Glencora, who rebel.

We feel restriction in more than sexual relations. It is difficult to imagine ourselves in a world where to pass to the social floor above you was a triumph and to fall to the floor below was disgraceful or comic. Again we forget that there existed then a very real difference in the background, training and associations of the classes which has by now long ceased to exist. The Education Act was not passed till 1870 ; the middle class had only exceptionally received the public school education of the upper class, until Dr. Arnold reformed the public schools in the middle of the century. Interests, occupations, the use of leisure, the content of conversation differed from class to class. It was difficult for the Victorians to conceive that a common national culture could ever envelop all individuals ; that it would be possible for a ploughman eventually to assimilate the associations and manners reserved at that time for the peer. Even Trollope writes in his Autobiography, speaking of the Civil Service examinations, " It may be that the son of the butcher of the village shall become as well fitted for employments requiring gentle culture as the son of the parson. Such is often the case . . . but the chances are greatly in favour of the parson's son . . . no good can be done by declaring that there . . . [is] no difference."

Restriction of movement operated also in the sphere of profession. The Church, the Services, the Bar, Politics and Business (if large enough) were acceptable professions for a young man who did not want to demean himself. He could also be a gentleman farmer interested in scientific methods (apart, that is, from being a landowner, which was a position above reproach, but one conferred by fate rather than sought). Colonial administration in the higher grades was gentlemanly—though novelists rather unfairly considered it fit for duffers only. Doctors just scraped through if successful enough and journalism was only possible to those who were either so blue blooded or so eccentric that their profession need not be taken seriously. Artists, like doctors, were accepted only if successful. The Civil Service was possible in its higher ranks but the lower ranks were socially obscure. If a young man needed money and had no aptitude for any of these professions he was in a desperate position. Racing, gaming and borrowing money on note of hand seemed the only way out. If he did not need money it was perfectly honourable to do nothing at all—this is, perhaps, the aspect of Victorian social life most difficult for us to understand.

The snobbery of the age is only too well known to us ; it is amply covered by contemporary writers as well as by those who came after them. It was an inevitable effect of the sudden social changes that had taken place with the industrial revolution and the first Reform Bill and although amusing for us it is not quite so important a vice as has been

implied. We, in fact, can be thankful for it : few weaknesses lend themselves to such delicious satire as snobbery
if delicately handled. It was not always so handled ; a
good number of writers of the time were inverted snobs
and spoilt their own wickets. Trollope was not only
not a snob, but he was not an inverted snob either ; the
subtlety of his satire is unsurpassed in the fiction of the
time.

Behind these conventions and attitudes, not always
penetrating personal conduct and thought, seldom vitalising
action, but nevertheless always there, a backcloth to life,
was religion, represented to most either by the Established
Church or by Dissent. Formal religion was at least as personally important as politics to the average man or woman ;
in many cases, particularly in smaller communities, a great
deal more so. It was also deeply mixed up with politics ;
the triumph of the Whigs in the 1830s was due to the Dissenting vote ; Radical and Dissenter were almost synonymous
terms of abuse to the other side. It was largely the dissenting
part of the population that had imposed such an iron law of
social " morality " ; the dissenters, aided by the Evangelicals
and Low Church supporters introduced a hell-fire element,
a Roundhead hatred of gaiety, ritual and tolerance. The
average Church of England member hated the drabness of
Dissent, resented their break with tradition and feared their
politics. Trollope himself was a Whig, but he was far from
being a Radical and he took a perfectly conventional
" established " view of Dissent and the Low Churchmen.
In this respect he showed no detachment from contemporary
prejudice. He resented drabness and, extrovert as he was,
suspected any creed which seemed to him to lay more stress
on faith than on works.

Meanwhile the Church of England was struggling with troubles within her own house. She had carried into the nineteenth century a dubious reputation for tolerating sinecures, dragging wealthy and idle cathedral clergy uncritically along, leaving poor curates to starve ; her concern with the spiritual welfare of the people had almost ceased to be perceptible. This was all changed by the middle of the century ; there had been a redistribution of clerical wealth, sinecures had come under fierce attack (*The Warden* gives a picture of this) and most important, the spiritual vigour of the Church had been revived by the Oxford Movement. Nevertheless, she still had to contend with warring parties inside—Low Churchmen and High— and the battle was joined by the public, who, if religion had little meaning in terms of spiritual values as we understand them, looked on forms of doctrine and observance as part of national life and considered any meddling with them to be, in some obscure way, a threat to their liberties. It is a sign of the importance religious forms held for the people that statesmen were alternately obliged to appease Dissent and Establishment, and had to be susceptible to the claims of both, as expressed politically or socially.

In fact, most of the great reformers were Dissenters or Evangelicals (Lord Shaftesbury, for instance, was an Evangelical) ; the Dissenting Whig was frequently a Liberal in international affairs, non-insular, idealistic. For this reason they were looked on with contempt and suspicion by the middle-class, Established Church members, who thought them little better than traitors. " The cotton spinners' babble," " the ignoble doctrines of Manchester " shocked Meredith's Everard Romfrey—doughty son of a race of fighting earls—when the Radicals repudiated a warlike reply to French insults, in the opening of *Beauchamp's Career*.

The conception of "land" was an extremely significant factor in the nineteenth-century attitude of mind. In 1851, the census showed that half the population was rural, half urban. The growth of town life had been astoundingly rapid since the opening of the century, but even so the balance lay even and the particular twist which an urban economy and urban manners give to a country was not yet typical in England. Two social systems existed; the rural-aristocratic in the country, the mercantile-democratic in the city. The counties were still, in the middle of the century, ruled by the local landowner; the cities' municipal councils came from the rising class. It was not till the last quarter of the century that the decay of agriculture set in and the influence of landlords and farmers began to wane, never to revive again. But at no time during the reign of the great Victorian novelists was there any doubt that the possession of land was the ultimate good for an Englishman—something between a vocation and a divine trust. The possession of land, held through centuries, enabled a commoner of good blood to look anyone in the face; to take a strong line about receiving recent peers and industrial millionaires in his house. As land was lost, through bad luck, debt or recklessness, so the very stature of a man seemed to himself to shrink. A man had some virtue from the very land he held, as though he were thereby made part of England.

Behind the scenes of city life, the Mayfair drawing-rooms and the dark libraries of city merchants and lawyers in Bloomsbury, behind the festivities of the Piccadilly clubs and the hurry of Fleet Street, always, in the Victorian novel, and above all in the novels of Trollope, one must be aware, as the writers were, of the great stretches of downland, meadow, parkland, ploughed field, moor and wood which lapped London round, and of the lives that were lived among them ; the lives of the farmer, the squire and the large landowner and, equally, the lives of those who tended the lands they held from them. These continued to maintain a pattern of life which had existed before the factory chimneys had risen ; a pattern of life and thought which was still—though it was not to be for much longer—essentially representative of English thinking and English life.

Finally there is one social circumstance which should be kept in mind, since money and marriage are the two chief themes of Victorian novels and are among the chief themes of Trollope's. Until The Married Women's Property Acts a man secured a fortune for himself by marrying a rich wife ; marrying her took the place—no bones were made about it—of a profession. Conversely, a woman was dependent on her husband, except in so far as a legal settlement was made at marriage. Another financial point to bear in mind is that Members of Parliament were paid no salary till long after Trollope's death. In order to enter Parliament it was necessary to have an independent income. For a professional man it meant a financial sacrifice ; but it was to many a patriotic ideal to represent the country, and to many a social triumph. What money could not give, you might achieve, in prestige and social advancement, by going to Westminster.

It was the age of the Philistines ; yet it was in this age that modern democracy was realised in England ; through the Reform Bills, through the Factory Acts, through the Education Act, through the recognition of the Trade Unions. At this time the ground was prepared for the phenomenal sweep of social legislation in the early twentieth century.

In no country had there ever been such a deliberate and
steady advance towards achieving equality before the law,
equality in opportunity and in political representation.
At no time before, or in any other country, had man's recognition of what is due to man been so fully accepted as the
motive for legislation.   Changes—changes too great to be
easily digestible—had come and these changes had brought
injustices ;   poverty to thousands as well as wealth to
hundreds.   Struggling to adjust matters, the middle classes
of England dealt earnestly with the injustices, in the way
they knew best—by legislation to lighten misery, by found-
ing papers to air grievances, by establishing charities to
patch up the wrecks.

If we look at their world from our distance, it seems, for
all its crassness and stupidities to have done pretty well.   But
if, like a moving camera, we could travel back to a close-up,
we would notice that the steady roar and bump of production, the steady hum of voices passing progressive legislation were interrupted by cries and struggles, not from the
industrialists or the legislators, but from others.

The agony of those cries was very great ;   for it was the
agony of men calling on men to cease from blasphemy.
Dante's horror and pity at observing the particular hells
for particular sinners was not greater than the pity and horror
of certain men as they watched England preparing her own
hell for herself.   They believed that the people of England
had sold all the hours of their days to the productive machine ;
but of man's life, the machine required only a part—the
rest was thrown out as inconsumable, as slag.   But this
slag, protested the thinking men, this waste matter, was,
in fact, the element that made humanity human, indeed,
divine.

These onlookers—philosophers, poets, writers and theologians—were not opposed to machinery as such ; what disgusted and frightened them was the way in which men were falling for the machine and above all, for the economy that the machine had made possible, if not inevitable. The age had produced its own ethos, an ethos which comprehended neither good nor evil but only automatic movement. The gospel of the new order, as preached by the economists, was magnetising. It was true—you could see it working ; it was neat, logical and sufficient. It had, too, a kind of grandeur ; it dealt objectively with the world and in comprehensible abstracts—commodity, value, market, labour. It had the sureness, without the rather grim implications, of predestination. It dealt with things in bulk—men, goods, capacity—and, dealt with in bulk, all sorts of things were acceptable : the desperate competition of working-class families to work for the lowest wages, the starvation of those who lost in the game, the increasing power and wealth of those who gained control of the machine. All this, and more, could be accepted because no one was personally responsible ; the laws which operated the system were beyond human control. Supply and Demand, the Law of Self Interest and the rest put the machine into motion and kept it going.

It was the economic ideology, and its merciless conception of man's destiny that anguished and angered the humanists of the century. And though, throughout their time, the noise of the machine is loud, their voices are louder still. Countering the firm tones of the economists come the denunciations, bitter or grieving, of Froude, Newman, Ruskin, Carlyle and, later, the earnest appeals of Morris and the suave sophisticated denigrations of Arnold. They call on their fellow-men to stop for a moment, to remember something and above all, to think. But they are scarcely understood. Some large degree of apprehension has been lost and will not be regained for many years. Values have been misplaced. The wrong objects have been priced and it is difficult to remember where the right objects have gone— or what they were.

So Emerson, visiting us from the brave New World, wrote of the English, " They are impious in their scepticism of theory and in high departments they are cramped and sterile. But the unconditional surrender to facts and their choice of means to reach their ends are as admirable as with ants and bees. The bias of the nation is a passion for utility."

This sterility of desire left the new rising class with uneasiness and restlessness of heart. They were not happy. They could not live greatly—there was no time. But many of them were anxious about themselves ; they eagerly read the great writers and took a kind of delight in hearing themselves denounced. They were a nostalgic people— only a generation removed from a quieter, smaller England which lived, taken by and large, by the precepts of the Bible. Where were they now ?

Matthew Arnold, in his imaginary conversation with the refractory foreign critics, quotes a contemporary statesman's boast, " The seven Houses of Commons that have sate since the Reform Bill have performed exploits unrivalled, not merely in the six centuries during which Parliament has existed, but in the whole history of representative assemblies." But his critics are not impressed. " What is the modern problem ? " They (or rather Arnold) reply, " To make human life, the life of society, all through, more natural and rational ; to have the greatest possible number of one's nation happy. . . . What do you make of the mass of your society. . . . Are you a success with your middle class? They have the power now; what have they made of themselves? . . . The fineness and capacity of a man's spirit is shown by his enjoyments . . . drugged with business, your middle class seems to have its sense blunted for any stimulus besides, except religion; it has a religion, narrow, unintelligent, repulsive. . . . What other enjoyments have they? . . . A literature of books . . . utterly unreadable by an educated class anywhere . . . and in their evenings, for a great treat, a lecture on teetotalism or nunneries. . . . The middle class . . . possesses life only by reading in the newspapers, which it does devoutly, the doings of great people."

Yet gentleness and sensitivity and high purpose did return to national life, emerging after a long period from the darkness imposed by industrial expediency. The future is not so easily sold away as the present. Trollope, a man less sensitive and less cultured than Arnold, had nevertheless a humbler view of what a generation could accomplish either for good or ill. He was consequently a greater optimist. A few years before Arnold wrote this passage in *Friendship's Garland*, Trollope had written:

We are always in such a hurry; although as regards the progress of races, history so plainly tells us how vain such hurry is! At thirty, a man devotes himself to proselytising a people; and if the people be not proselyted when he has reached forty, he retires in disgust. . . . The process has been too long. The nation should have risen free, at once, upon the instant. It is hard for man to work without hope of seeing that for which he labours. . . . Men are in such a hurry. They can hardly believe that that will come to pass of which they have evidence that it will not come to pass in their own days.

## II

LOOKING at Trollope's work against the background of his time we should concede that he had prejudices which we cannot share (we have not always the same provocation). He disliked Dissenters ; he tended to patronise Radicals—whom he described simply as demagogues, *vide* Mr. Turnbull in *Phineas Finn* ; his acceptance of the fullest obligations of the marriage tie seems to us often to be unenlightened in view of the cruelties which he knew to exist in certain marriages. That he was not wholly free of the narrow " morality " of his time we can guess by his treatment of some of his lighthearted and witty characters and by the suspicion we get that his people are generally morally safer in the country than in the town ; that he had been affected by the commercial ethic of the time we detect by a slight tendency to identify propriety with prudence in dealing with love affairs. The arguments advanced by his characters on behalf of a virtuous suitor tend to lay as much stress on his financial as his moral worthiness ; see how similar, in *Ayala's Angel,* are the arguments made to Ayala on behalf of her rich cousin, Tom, by her uncle, Sir Thomas Tringle, her Aunt Dosett and her girl friend Nina.

On the other hand, having enumerated his prejudices, the reader generally finds that Trollope had gone around the back way, as it were, to take the weight out of the charges. He patronised the young labour leader Ontario Moggs, in *Ralph the Heir,* but in *The Vicar of Bullhampton* he treats Mrs. Brattle with a moving and beautiful dignity and accords to her inarticulate distress an understanding which few writers accord to characters they do not consider to be their intellectual equals. Trollope's implicit insistence that we accept Mrs. Brattle on our own ground is of greater significance as a clue to his social ideas than his rough and ready treatment of Moggs's political philosophy—a philosophy he understood far less acutely than Disraeli. But Disraeli, for all his noble artisans, never drew a human being like Mrs. Brattle. And if Trollope accepted the cruel penalties of the time for loosening the marriage tie, he could, on the other hand, describe the mental cruelties which can be inflicted within marriage with a keenness which surely evokes thoughtful consideration of what domestic tyranny can be.

He had no illusions about the importance to marriage of comfort and of a common background. (" A man," he writes in *The Three Clerks,* " in taking a wife from any rank much below his own . . . will have to endure habits, manners and ideas which the close contiguity of married life will force upon his disgusted palate, which must banish all love.") But if he had no false romanticism about love as a substitute for amenities, neither did he have any illusions about rank or money as substitutes for love. Who could write so skilfully of the bitterness of a purely " convenient " marriage, as for instance, in the story of Lady Laura Kennedy in *Phineas Finn* or of Crosbie in *The Small House at Allington* ; Or the danger of pulling apart a couple whose marriage is merely financially unsuitable, as in the story of Mary Lowther in *The Vicar of Bullhampton* ?

And though, again, he allowed himself the insularities of the Englishmen of his time, so that, indeed, his pictures of foreigners are patronising at the worst and comic at the best (and his foreign stories seldom more than charming little trivialities), yet from his heart he can write to his American friend, Kate Field, " One is patriotic only because one is too small and weak to be cosmopolitan."

Trollope's prejudices are of minor importance to his writing because they were not supremely important to him. He is interested in the fundamental sources of evil which lie in the heart, rather than in their social manifestations. His dislike of Low Church bigotry (as he saw it) has been mentioned ; yet it is notable that in *John Caldigate* which contains a study of a bigoted Low Church woman, he attributes Mrs. Bolton's cruelty not primarily to her religion but to her desire for domination, for which she uses her religion as an excuse.

It is this approach, the human approach rather than the social, which gives his work as a novelist, continuing validity ; but it was this approach which put him at odds with the great thinkers of his time. He could not generalise as they could—as they must generalise to drive their lesson home. He could only see the world in terms of individuals. He reacted irritably to their upbraidings, scarcely conscious that he was preaching, in the concrete and the particular, against the very things which they were condemning in the abstract and the general.

> Can a world, retrograding from day to day in honesty, be considered to be in a state of progress. We know the opinion on this subject of our philosopher Mr. Carlyle. If he be right, we are all going straight away to darkness and the dogs. But then we do not put very much faith in Mr. Carlyle —nor in Mr. Ruskin and his other followers. The loudness and extravagance of their lamentations, the wailing and gnashing of teeth which comes from them . . . are so contrary to the convictions of men who cannot but see how comfort has been increased, how health has been improved and

education extended—that the general effect of their teaching is
the opposite of what they have intended. . . . It is Carlyleism
to opine that the general grand result of increased intelligence
is a tendency to deterioration.

So he writes in his Autobiography when speaking of the
disgust with his age which impelled him to start on his
great satire, *The Way We Live Now*, a satire which aptly
illustrated all that these men had been preaching ! As a
man who was professionally a Civil Servant—a member of
that Service which translates the abstracts of freedom,
enlightenment and education into the dull concretes of
legislation—he enjoyed assuming stupidity about metaphors
and grand periods of speech and asking what they meant.
A delicious, if rather shocking example of this can be found
in his review of Ruskin's *Crown of Wild Olive* in the
*Fortnightly Review* (Vol. V, 1866).

In fact, Trollope's direct approach to objects or experience
often had a surprising effect on his point of view on general
affairs. His opinions, however, were delivered in such a
commonplace fashion, so utterly without rodomontade,
that they never fluttered the dovecots—and it was the doves
and not the eagles for whom he wrote. This is a passage
from his book on the West Indies, which he considered one
of his best works.

> I shall be certain in speaking of the coloured men to offend
> my friends in Jamaica . . . they look on themselves as the
> ascendant race. I look upon those of colour [1] as being so, or
> at least as about to become so. . . . I believe that the light of
> their [the white] star is waning, that their ascendancy is over.
> . . . Ascendancy is a disagreeable word to apply to any two
> different races whose fate it may be to live together in the same
> land . . . but nevertheless . . . when two rivers come

[1] i.e. mixed race.

together, the waters of which do not mix, the one stream will be the stronger . . . the coloured men of Jamaica cannot be despised much longer. It will be said that we have been wrong if we have ever despised these coloured people, or indeed, if we have ever despised the negroes, or any other coloured race. I can hardly think that anything so natural can be very wrong. Those who are educated and civilised and powerful will always, in one sense, despise those who are not . . . if the coloured people in the West Indies can overtop contempt, it is because they are acquiring education, civilization and power. In Jamaica they are, I hope, in a way to do this. . . . The necessary compound [of European, Asian and African blood] will be formed for these latitudes.

Many implications in this—the suggestions that mis-cegenation was a positive good, that a coloured race could and should displace the Anglo-Saxon, that the English domin-ation should give way to other races progressively throughout the world (which point he enlarges on in other parts of the book), might be considered risky to lay before a Victorian public. But he makes no concessions to us either. " I hardly think that anything so natural can be very wrong." In any age people are apt to be jarred by a perfectly straight acceptance of things as they are and to re-state the facts with current knobs on. Trollope is rare among writers in this ; that he admitted to his mind no more than he could swear to the truth of.

If this is the case with Trollope, his achievement as a writer depended on the width of his experience on the one hand, and the depth of his imaginative capacity on the other—on his capacity for extracting significance from experience.

There was, at least, nothing limited about his experience. In childhood and youth he endured poverty of the most humiliating and spiritually degrading kind. In early manhood he knew, first, shame and frustration, but he slowly learnt to do a job well, to accomplish what he set out to do and to insist on recognition. He travelled over most of Europe, to the New World and to what were then the Colonies. He married—happily—had children, learned how to make the friends he most wished to have, after years of unpopularity. He emerged from obscurity to social success. He lived in the city and in the country. He rose nearly to the top of his profession in the Civil Service and at the same time he wrote over eighty books. He suffered literary failure and enjoyed phenomenal literary success. He stood for Parliament but failed to get in. He conducted important negotiations as an official on behalf of his country. Nothing that life offered him did he refuse ; his faculties were stretched out for experience ; movement, change, feeling of any kind were for him positive things and therefore to be desired. He pursued life with the same eagerness as he pursued the fox, neither did he shrink from mental pain or from the melancholia that often overcame him any more than he sacrificed his joy of hunting because he was nearly blind or because he knew that the long ride back would nearly always bring with it a fearful depression of spirits.

Trollope's experience, however, had a greater content even than appears, because he never ceased actively to receive impressions ; he was always registering. An Irish-woman told his biographer, Escott, that Trollope's close looking into objects reminded her of a woman in a shop examining materials for a new dress. He did not only look closely at the tangible world ; he directed the same concentrated gaze on conduct and on men's reactions to each other.

A.T.—3

As far as experience of living was concerned, Trollope was as well qualified as any writer for his job. Was the capacity of his imagination great enough to use experience as a great writer can ? This is a question which cannot be so directly answered. We might say—Trollope's imaginative capacity made him a great novelist ; but a great writer is something more than that.

He lacked any touch of the metaphysical. He was not even interested in ideas as such, but only in ideas as they could be, as it were, synthesised from human action. He was more aware of the world than of the universe. He was an enormous reader but, as we have seen, he thinks little of the greatest writers of his day. Of the French or German philosophers he never says a word. He had a reverent love of poetry but his comments on poetry are conventional. From five o'clock in the morning till late at night he was occupied with something every day of his adult life ; but there is no indication that he ever read for the sake of projecting himself into a world of which he was not already possessed. There is a revealing sentence in his critique of Thackeray. Speaking of himself he says, " I was told that I ought to go home, drink tea and read good books. It was excellent advice but I found that the reading of good books and solitude was not an occupation congenial to me."

One approaches this question of Trollope's imaginative—or perhaps spiritual—capacity cautiously and by a series of negatives because no one who has read the bulk of his books could be sure that a quality, beyond the quality required by a great novelist, did not exist behind his alert, intent eyes. One cannot be sure that the delicacy, the pity and the occasional grandeurs of some of his novels could have been conceived by any but an artist of greater scope than Trollope ever claimed to be. Some clue to this may be found in *The Macdermots of Ballycloran*, his first book.

He was twenty-eight when he began this book in 1843, and had been stationed in Ireland for two years. He had here found his feet in the Civil Service and had emerged from the "years of suffering, disgrace and inward remorse" which had enveloped him from infancy. A publisher friend of his mother's brought the book out, but Trollope received no money from it and it was never reviewed. " I was sure," he wrote in middle age, " that it would fail and it did fail most absolutely."

*The Macdermots* is a remarkable piece of work if considered simply as the first novel of a young man whose life had been as sterile as had Trollope's till that time. It has all the qualities of close observation, sympathy and humour which he was to develop so widely later on. Its characters are well conceived, the suspense is well maintained. It is the story of a broken-down Irish landowning family and the end of the last members of it—in madness, on the gallows and in shameful death. The period is the Ireland of the 1840s, just before the Famine.

What is remarkable about this book, however, is that it has a kind of poetic power and sense of fate which never appear so explicitly again in his works. It is not a great book, but it is the book of a man who may write great books later—the book, in fact, of an incipient great writer as distinct from a great novelist. What is called in music " the dynamics " are on a great scale, and the placing of the characters against fate, the struggle of the inarticulate, the oppressed and the bewildered against outside forces are at least distantly reminiscent of the conflicts of Greek drama and

Russian fiction. Trollope's job in Ireland turned him from a Civil Service failure to a Civil Service success ; socially and mentally the country unlocked him and enabled him to fulfil himself. But it also stimulated some inner source of feeling which was fully awakened by no other place or society. It is significant that he returned to Ireland for material for his last book, *The Land Leaguers*—indeed this visit and the fatigues it cost him are thought to have precipitated his death.

There are signs, in his youthful work, of the pull in the author's mind between poetic imagination on the one side and the pleasures of sheer observation on the other : by the end of the story, observation has become the vehicle for tragedy—feeling is stronger than events. Such a victory was never again so decisive in Trollope's books.

Why was this ? Perhaps there is one answer in his Autobiography. " My first manuscript I gave up to my mother, agreeing with her that it would be as well that she should not look at it before she gave it to a publisher. I knew that she did not give me credit for the sort of cleverness necessary for such work. I could see in the faces and hear in the voices of . . . my friends . . . my mother, my sister, my brother-in-law and, I think, my brother—that they had not expected me to come out as one of the family authors. There were three or four in the field before me . . . I could perceive that this attempt of mine was felt to be an unfortunate aggravation of the disease."

He followed *The Macdermots* by another novel of Irish life, less striking, and by an undistinguished French historical novel. It was not till nine years after the commencement of *The Macdermots*, when he was back in England, an established and esteemed official, that he began *The Warden*,

the first of the Trollope novels as most of his public think
of them, and the first of his books for which he received
payment.

His own comment on *The Macdermots* is, " As to the plot
itself, I do not know that I ever made one so good—or, at
any rate, one so susceptible of pathos.  I am aware that
I broke down in the telling, not having yet studied the art.
Nevertheless, *The Macdermots* is a good novel." " Pathos "
is a word which Trollope used seriously, applying it, often,
as a test of merit.  Its flavour has thinned a little lately, and
has tended to become associated with dogs and little children.
But for Trollope the word had power, retaining its Greek
origin.

The incident of *The Macdermots* has been dwelt on at
length because it points to depths of quality in Trollope's
works which have been ignored.  This deeper quality,
whatever it is, was forced through smaller vents in later
books, but there is a magnitude in his best work—*The Prime
Minister, The Last Chronicle, The Way We Live Now,* to
take three examples only—which it is hard to believe could
have been apprehended by a purely objective, or let us simply
say, a purely comedy writer.  There is no explicit sign to
show us whether Trollope himself believed himself possessed
of more than a good novelist's powers, though there is
one possibly disingenuous remark in his critique on Thackeray
which may be revealing.  " The object of a novel should
be to instruct in morals while it amuses . . . whether this
may be done by the transcendental or the commonplace
is a question which it more behoves the reader rather than
the author to answer ;  because the author may be fairly
sure that he who can do the one will not, probably cannot,
do the other."  But it must be remembered that Trollope

was very much out of patience with arty talk. His, to us, admirable swing to what he calls " the commonplace " may be something of a reaction to early manifestations of " art for art's sake." What he knew of his inner self, what he had repressed or expelled, he was determined to keep to himself. His view of his own popularity is so objective as to be almost sardonic.[1]

But this we do know ; that public taste leaped to *Barchester Towers* and has never detached itself from the Barsetshire series. Ever since the day he wrote the story of Mrs. Proudie and Mr. Slope, Trollope has been considered the novelist of the comedy of manners, the perfect bed-book writer. For every ten who have read *Barchester Towers* there is probably one who has read *The Prime Minister* and scarcely one in twenty has read *The Way We Live Now*. Even *The Last Chronicle*—the greatest of the Barsetshires—is far less popular than the others. Yet perfect as are the Barsetshires in their perception, their comedy, their variety of character and, above all, in the maintenance of suspense and in the sharpness of their focal scenes, they have not— with the exception of *The Last Chronicle*—the stature of later books, the political novels, for instance. They deal with what concerns the human day ; but these others deal with what concerns human life.

The tide of Trollope's popularity carried his books on the flood till nearly the end of his life ; even so *The Prime Minister* was a failure, and its unsuccess hurt him badly. He was not to be allowed by his public to go beyond the bounds of a certain kind of comedy, to rise above a certain level of

---

[1] Before closing all discussion of Trollope's awareness of the metaphysical, or poetic, world, let us not forget the sunset passage from the chapter " The Arm in the Clouds," in his slight but charming novel, *Rachel Ray*.

intensity. Trollope has suffered, perhaps more than most novelists, from a reputation arising less from the quality of his work as a whole, than from the public's taste for particular works. To-day, even, he is suffering from the same limitations on his popularity that he suffered from nearly a hundred years ago. To-day he has a potential public for what—it is reasonable to believe—he himself rightly considered the best qualities in all his works : but the very virtues of *Barchester Towers* are still obscuring the achievements of even greater books.

# III

IN considering Trollope's potential capacity as a writer, one at once comes up against the question of his style. It is his style which gives him his reputation as a basically unserious writer. He seems to have surrendered without a struggle to a purely narrative style, as though he had early in his writing career—when his family smiled at his efforts perhaps—decided that he was cut out for no more than a story-teller. In nothing that he wrote—except possibly in the Autobiography—did he divest himself of his particular leisurely, untense diction. He had no idiosyncrasies and no verbal dramatics. His style, for all its ease, was tyrannical ; it resisted any effort to tauten, compress or supercharge it. His attempts to write anonymously—in *Linda Tressel* and *Nina Balatka*—were quite unsuccessful. A pointed example of the inescapably narrative character of his writing can be seen in his biography of Palmerston. Here he is dealing with fact, with a man he understood in a time he knew ; it was an opportunity for " serious " writing and clearly Trollope did not intend the book as a frivolous work. It is most readable ; witty, shrewd, honest and revealing, all in all, a penetrating appraisal of Palmerston as a man and as a statesman. But one has, while reading it, the curious sensation that one is dealing with fiction—with, in fact, one of Trollope's own political novels. This is due not to the matter, but to the manner of the book. For instance :

> The circumstances of his going were of a nature to bring about a violent decision of the Catholic claims, though it cannot be said that he himself was in any way responsible for doing

so. There came up some dispute of East Retford and Penrhyn, in the course of which Mr. Huskisson resigned. Mr. Huskisson was a follower of Mr. Canning. That the Duke and Mr. Huskisson should not have been easy together in the same Cabinet we can understand ; but we are told that Mr. Huskisson was anxious that his resignation should not be accepted. The Duke, however, was determined that he should go, and would hear nothing of any mistake made as to the letter of resignation.

Or,

During these eighteen years he was thoroughly learning his duty as a Minister of the Crown—learning, as some will say, how to exaggerate those duties, and to absorb into his own hands more of power and potentiality than had been intended by those who had appointed him. But by himself, though he thought probably but little about it while he was learning it, the lesson had to be learned ; and the lesson taught seems to have been this, that he would interfere with the duties of no other office than his own, but with those duties he would put up with no interference. There may have been danger in this ; but such was his theory of official life.

This is fact. Here is fiction, from *The Eustace Diamonds* :

She had been a very clever child, a clever, crafty child ; and now she was becoming a clever woman. Her craft remained with her ; but so keen was her outlook upon the world, that she was beginning to perceive that craft, let it be never so crafty, will in the long run miss its own object. She actually envied the simplicity of Lucy Morris. . . . But she could see—or half see—that Lucy with her simplicity was stronger than was she with her craft. She had nearly captivated Frank Greystock with her wiles, but without any wiles Lucy had captivated him altogether.

The cadence, the approach to the sentence climax, is the same in each book ; there is the same repetition of a word, the same picking up and carrying on from one short clause to the next, so that we have the feeling of continually going back a step before we go forward. There is, in the fact as in the fiction, the same gusto, the same anecdotal air, " There came up some dispute of East Retford and Penrhyn," " That Mr. Huskisson and the Duke should not have been easy together we can understand." Now this relaxed approach, this method of tentatively setting down a statement and then circling around it, this intoxication with repetition, can be used for weaving a fabric but not for building great structures or for shooting at a mark. It is organically impossible, with such a style, to wind up a sprung thought within a sentence and release it.

These were, however, the only cadences in which Trollope seems to have been able to write ; and in reading some of his more deeply charged descriptive or meditative passages, one is inclined to feel that his style was too weak to support his imagination, rather than that his imagination was too restricted to inflate his style. His diction served him wonderfully well on the plains but it could not carry him up the mountains. Being primarily a man of feeling rather than a poet or philosopher, he found this unforced narrative style which came so easily to him, a perfect vehicle for what he thought himself fitted to do. We are left wondering whether he was not a little greater than he thought.

Whatever may be the disadvantages of his style, it is admirable for narrative ; in the enormous bulk of his work [1] there are scarcely a dozen books which are not intensely readable from start to finish. This very readability has acted against his reputation ; it is difficult to read him critically because he is so entrancing a story-teller—anticipation cannot wait on analysis. How he contrived to maintain suspense with so relaxed a style of writing, it is difficult to

[1] He wrote eighty novels—apart from short stories and non-fiction work.

explain ; but perhaps a good deal by his very method of going back to go forward. Each sentence, each paragraph, is left to be " continued in our next " ; new streams of suggestion join the main current of thought with every clause ; each amplification takes one deeper into the situation, creating thereby, an opening for new action. The secret of Trollope's style, in fact, is movement, and this preoccupation with movement accounts both for his achievement and for his weakness : for there must be some static quality about abstract thought or poetic power, while, on the other hand, a writer cannot reproduce life unless he has a real feeling for change, for progression—a feeling which will inform his actual sentence construction.

Trollope's own views on what a novel should be and how a writer should handle his material is set out fully in his Autobiography (a book which is outstanding among his works). Plot, style, the drawing of character, the proper method of working (so many words to so many lines each day) is there discussed in his own direct, engaging way. It makes not only interesting but useful reading. Though it appears to amount only to this ; be absolutely truthful ; study how to avoid tedium ; immerse yourself in the lives of your characters ; never relax in observation ; study proportion ; teach what is good ; be industrious. The many pages on the art of novel-writing are a fascinating guide to Trollope's conscious values ; they make up a useful textbook of rules on workmanship. " The ordinary talk of educated people is carried on in short sharp expressive sentences, which very frequently are never completed—the language of which, even among educated people, is often incorrect. The novel-writer in constructing his dialogue must so steer between absolute accuracy of language—which would give to his conversation an air of pedantry, and the slovenly inaccuracy of ordinary talkers, which, if closely followed, would offend by an appearance of grimace—as to produce upon the ear of his readers a sense of reality. If he be quite real he will seem to attempt to be funny. If he be quite correct he will seem to be unreal."

We get in these notes a glimpse of his passionate devotion to the trade of novel-writing. Speaking of characters, he says, " They must be with him [the writer] as he lies down to sleep, and as he wakes from his dreams. He must learn to hate them and to love them. He must argue with them, quarrel with them, forgive them and even submit to them." Here we get another clue to his strength and to his weakness in writing. His intense preoccupation with his created world, which made him reject anything which was not real, which was not true enough to be argued with, or valid enough to stand by itself. (So that the phrase " created world " seems scarcely the right one to use for the world of Trollope's books : Is Barsetshire a county and if not, by what terms is it unreal ?) All this demanded an absorption in what was around him. As he grew older and as the world became more receptive to him, he was swamped by the pleasures of observation and consequently by the urge to reproduce the thousand twists and turns of human life which he saw operating in their complex pattern between sunrise and sunset each day. There was enough to keep a man busy for all his life on what he could see in one day— how should he ever catch up with what could be seen and heard in a lifetime ? Irresistibly, he was drawn into daily life, and to its reproduction in his books he devoted an imagination which, at one time, had sent feelers out into a larger atmosphere.

And in order that others should enter into this world about them and understand its value as he did, he adopted a style which almost sucked them into his books ; there must be no barrier to their participation ; no difficulty should cause them to hesitate on the threshold. Greatness, for himself, might be lost—but what he had to tell was so important that personal greatness did not rank high beside it.

> The language used should be as ready and as efficient a conductor of the mind of the writer to the mind of the reader as is the electric spark which passes from one battery to another battery. In all written matter the spark should carry everything ; but in matters recondite the recipient will search to see that he misses nothing, and that he takes nothing away too much. The novelist cannot expect that any such search will be made. . . . Poetry takes the highest place . . . That nobility of expression and all but divine grace of words . . .. is not compatible with prose . . . the writer has soared above the earth and can teach his lessons somewhat as a god might teach. He who sits down to write his tale in prose makes no such attempt, nor does he dream that the poet's honour is within his reach.

Trollope's notes on writing, for all their honesty and shrewdness, do not really explain his secret. If we look for an answer from him as to exactly how he managed his craft so as to achieve more than good craftsmanship, we feel as unsatisfied as did the young dancer who asked Nijinsky how he managed his famous leaps and was told, " You just leap into the air, stay there a little while and come down." He tells us to study proportion ; that a novel should not be episodic—or rather, that every episode should be organic ; that the characters should grow within the book. But this cannot explain how he so skilfully selects the moments of action on which to forward his story, the faultless way he cuts in on his characters' lives, the details he picks up to furnish his world. He tells how to construct dialogue and advises a writer to live with his characters, but leaves untold the secret of informing perfectly trivial dialogue with poignancy—a poignancy so implicit that it is possible to search over and over again through a passage without finding the word or phrase which actually carries the significance of the scene. This hidden significance makes Trollope an almost unquotable writer ; it is necessary to read through an entire book to get the full emotional content of any passage, since each carries within it the accumulated emotion of past experience. To point up the moment, Trollope gives only a hint—sometimes no more than a single adjective or adverb—to indicate its focal value. But the reader is by now so charged with experience that this hint acts as a catharsis ; a flow of feeling is released. Trollope has his way with us—without, apparently, lifting a finger.

# IV

ALTHOUGH Trollope was in a sense an "automatic" writer, receiving the world directly and directly transcribing what he saw, he was an artist in that he made this material significant; his work added up to something. He was an artist, too, in that he explored and to a large extent made his own, a particular level on which people live their lives—the level of conduct and behaviour. He used conduct for his interpretation of life. This had been done before, of course, specifically, by Jane Austen—a writer he very deeply admired—and it is being done to-day by E. M. Forster and Elizabeth Bowen; and although he is less of an artist than any of these three, it is with such writers as these, rather than with writers of passion and "event" that he should fairly be compared.

Trollope was interested—if one can use so deliberate a word—in how far the internal realities of peoples' natures, their strengths, weaknesses, courage, ambition, fidelity, rapacity and so on, are carried onto the external levels on which behaviour has play—how far every relation and exchange between one human being and another is affected by these fundamental qualities at this level. His skill is shown in this; that at all times this level is perfectly maintained. He never cheats: at no time is character made to serve plot, or is plot distorted to maintain character. Yet while staying within the limits of behaviour and adjusting his treatment most delicately to this particular pitch among the many on which life is expressed, he implies much of life that lies above and below behaviour and there arises therefore from his work a comprehension of what is noble, dignified and admirable in men and women.

By taking this level of living as his sphere, he cut himself off from nearly all adventitious aids. He most deliberately stuck to the normal ; he would not touch the unlikely, the eccentric—the character created for its own sake. This device appeared to him to be unworthy. For this reason he could not wholly admire Dickens. " I do acknowledge that Mrs. Gamp, Micawber, Pecksniff and others have become household words in every house, as though they were human beings ; but to my judgment they are not human beings, nor are any of the characters human which Dickens has portrayed. It has been the peculiarity and the marvel of this man's power, that he has invested his puppets with a charm that has enabled him to dispense with human nature."

For the same reason he could not touch what might be called a grievance, or a social evil ; unless, that is, it was an evil arising from the weakness of human nature. There is practically no mention in his books of topical social evils— the condition of prisons, workhouses, orphanages, factories and such. Not only did the interpretation of life with which he was concerned exclude these matters, but to have brought them in would have been to have called on associated emotions which had not their source purely in the problems with which he was dealing. It would have been what he might have called a demagogue's trick. His aim, as an artist, was to deal with what is continuously true and for that reason he had to eschew what was not particular to his particular social scene. In *The Vicar of Bullhampton*, for instance, he takes up arms for " the fallen woman," but he inveighs less against the evils of institutions or of custom than against the evil of intolerance and ignorance which made the institutions possible.

Trollope's passionate interest in living, as distinct from Life, has given him a value which he could not foresee. We have come near to losing the art of living by intercourse ; conduct has almost ceased to be an art. Also life has become more restricted, paradoxically enough ; long office hours and long train journeys, on the one hand, and supplied amusements, on the other, have eaten into the time which was once laid out in the play of relationships. There is less time for slow growth, for the silent maturing of feeling. The incidents of love, travel, change of residence or work pass frequently and rapidly across our lives and reaction is shallow. Often enough we live on borrowed feelings having had no time or thought to nourish our own. Consequently, the individual who is articulate gets an inflated value and literature and living is often distended by the wind of exhibitionism—a manifestation which would have puzzled as well as disgusted Trollope. On the other hand, we feel lonely ; life is precarious in every sense, and we doubt if we are making the best of it while we have it. The greater the forces which control us and which we cannot control, the less we feel able to play out our lives—what is left for us to handle ? Reading Trollope we can know that life on the level of behaviour is now, as it ever was, entirely ours to handle and that, skilfully handled, it can provide a pattern of the most intricate and delightful and even dramatic kind : that this pattern is not only exciting to the participator as participator, but also as observer.

This is the lesson which Trollope taught : he did not know he was teaching it, although he insisted that he was a teacher and wrote his novels almost as a mission. " The novelist . . . must preach his sermons with the same purpose as the clergyman, and must have his own system of ethics," he writes in the Autobiography, and these sentiments recur often. " No man or woman with intellect sufficient to produce amusement, can go on from year to year spinning stories without the desire of teaching ; with no ambition of influencing readers for their good." (*Ralph the Heir*). But the lesson he thought himself to be teaching was not so remote after all from the lesson he actually taught. For the pleasures of behaviour are pleasures only in so far as behaviour is spiced and tempered with nobility—it is restraint and modesty, courage and endurance, selflessness and patience, which gives behaviour a shape and which makes men and women able to weave a pattern worth watching or participating in. This is why Trollope's villains are never tedious ; even when they are most worthless and despicable, one can see behind them the shadow of the balanced human beings they might have been.

Trollope's conversational style gives his books an appearance of uniformity ; in fact they differ so much in plot and circumstance that it is difficult to generalise about them. He can be said to have dealt with one class—if one includes in it the tradesman or the clerk, at one end, and the Dukes of Omnium and St. Bungay at the other. In fact he dealt also with the working class, but he never brought in the very poor as primary characters. As he touched every layer in the " middle " class, however, he can fairly be claimed to have covered as large an area of the British public as has ever been covered intensively by an English novelist. He also dealt with Americans, brilliantly, with Jews and in general with foreigners—the last least successfully. As for types and trades—he portrayed business men, aristocrats, politicians, Civil Servants, usurers, spinsters, widows, yeomen farmers, landed gentry, soldiers, lawyers, landladies, doctors, heiresses, self-made men, tradesmen, hunting men, journalists, innkeepers, clergy of all kinds—simply to take a handful that occurs to the mind at random and without mentioning the foreign stories. The word " portrayed " is used advisedly ; for he did not simply label his characters with a profession or status—their profession or status is part of them and the distinctive paraphernalia, house, residential district, club, social circle, is an integral part of the character's story. Few other English novelists had so complete an understanding of so many kinds of lives or, if they did, were so well able to use their knowledge for the proper development of their stories.

To find a theme common to Trollope's novels one has to search deeper than his choice of types or his plots and penetrate to a fundamental conflict which is repeated in nearly all his books. It is the conflict between what a man or woman wants and what they think they want. The story is the progress of the characters through misapprehensions to the final peace of mind which comes to them when they have found their fundamental desire. This pattern has variations. In some cases the characters achieve no peace of mind, for by the time they know what they want, it is beyond their reach : Adolphus Crosbie in his betrayal and subsequent pursuit of Lily Dale is an example of this. In other books, the characters see more or less clearly what they want and are by nature unable to achieve it : the mutual love of George Bertram and Caroline Waddington is frustrated by their own natures—against their own wills. In any case, the " happy ending " for Trollope is not the Victorian happy ending as Mr. Orwell so vividly describes it in his essay on Dickens, "a vision of a huge loving family of three or four generations, all crammed together in the same house and constantly multiplying like a bed of oysters," (*Critical Essays*). Such a notion of happiness was pure fantasy from Trollope's point of view. His happy ending was a kind of spiritual emancipation : a man and woman, having worked through uncertainties, either about their love or their lives, or both, reach a certainty. The final pledges are made, one feels, not only by the lovers to each other, but to life whose demands they have learned to accept, or to their own integrity which events have taught them to honour. It is significant that the "happy endings"—usual, but not invariable in Trollope's books— generally absorb more than a mere concluding chapter. He had an acute sense of tempo, and whereas the turbulence of the crisis is conveyed by scenes of swiftly succeeding action, attacks being directed on the characters not only frontally, but from the wings (thus bringing into play the apparently minor characters living remote from the scene of action at the opening of the book), so, as the waters slow down and widen out, the tension is gradually slackened, the quiet of domesticity, of the friendly social round, is reintroduced ; peace flows slowly in now that the disturbing element has been removed. Normality returns, but everyone is a little older and a little wiser. This "happy ending" promises no certain happiness but inward sureness—and this, possibly, was the only happiness which Trollope recognised as lasting.

The struggle which takes place in Trollope's novels between his characters' conflicting desires is approached at many different levels and through all kinds of problems. It is not always so clearly the theme underlying the main plot—

or what should better be called the title plot, since in fact there is little to choose in importance between the plot to which the title refers and the " subplot." This theme of inward conflict scarcely appears in *Barchester Towers*, his first popular success, which is almost pure comedy : that is to say that the characters there are nearly all completely given up to their dominating desire—in the main figures, a desire for power. They are, for the most part, ready formed figures, no longer developing. For this reason it is, although one of the books most entertaining to read, yet one of the less deeply interesting—it makes a shallower impact on the mind although it undoubtedly makes a lasting impact on the memory. Mrs. Proudie, the Archdeacon, the Signora and Mr. Slope are out to succeed and to put one over on the opposing party. The story is an account of their degree of failure or success. Only Mr. Harding, Trollope's own saint, gently holds his mirror to the human heart and makes his submission to circumstance without rancour, as he has done before and will do again.

The second Barsetshire, *Dr. Thorne*, is a more purely " plot " novel enriched by first-rate character-drawing and comedy, but in the third of the Barsetshire books, *Framley Parsonage*, the pattern is already clear. Here we have on the one hand, the worldly friendly young clergyman whose inclination towards sophisticated society conflicts with the demands which his calling makes upon his nature. This conflict is complicated, in Trollope's own subtle fashion, by the fact that the lures of the world seem to coincide with the need to prove his manhood, to assert his independence of his patroness, Lady Lufton. On the other hand, there is the inverted conflict between his sister Lucy and her lover's family ; Lucy knows that if she surrenders to Lufton before her worth is recognised by Lady Lufton she will lose a self-respect for which no attachment will compensate her. She counterbalances her brother Mark : through all her misery she retains a certainty, a kind of peace of mind which he uneasily misses even at the height of his social success.

*Framley Parsonage* was an important book in Trollope's development as a novel-writer. It is one of the most personal of the earlier works, not in the way that a previous book, *The Three Clerks*, was personal, that is as autobiography, but in so far as the Trollope slant on life, his ethic and his chief preoccupations can be seen surfacing here. It was an important book for him, for it was written at the request of Thackeray, whom he admired, for the first number of the *Cornhill Magazine* ; it gave him his first real entry into the literary life of London. His delight in the strategy of politics can be seen here in miniature ; his delight in the busy, minor comings and goings of village life ; his sense that trains and posts provide a dramatic element in living ; his understanding of the destroying effects of poverty ; his comprehension of villainy as human personality in defeat. *Framley Parsonage* provides, as it were, the seed bed for the political wisdom and political excitement of the later Parliamentary novels, for the anguish of *The Last Chronicle*, for the studies of worthlessness in *The Way We Live Now*. The love story, however, stands complete in itself, tender, mature and entertaining. Not only is Lucy Robarts one of the finest of his " quiet " heroines, but in Lord Lufton he created almost his only heroic young man—lacking the indecision and self-pity, to which, in his irony, he made nearly all his heroes subject.

The most frequent version of the conflict is that of the struggle between real self fulfilment and the desire to climb.

In *The Three Clerks,* Alaric sacrifices honesty to promotion ;
he is consumed by his ambition to get to the top of the tree.
But there is no real ease of spirit for him till he comes out of
prison and emigrates to Australia to start life at the bottom.
Adolphus Crosbie sacrifices marital happiness to the cheapest
kind of snobbery. He is a clever man and knows almost
immediately what he has done. He will live in perpetual
unease, a spiritually broken man. Frank Greystock, in *The
Eustace Diamonds,* nearly sacrifices his integrity, as represented
by his love for Lucy Morris, to his career. Greystock was a
man who, " could walk along the banks of the quiet trout-
giving Bob, at Bobsborough . . . telling himself that the
world well lost for love would be a bad thing lost for a good
purpose ; who could also stand with his hands in his trousers'
pockets, looking down at the pavement, in the purlieus of
the courts at Westminster and swear to himself that he would
win the game, let the cost to his heart be what it might."
He needs money in order to afford to sit in Parliament ;
he burns to be a legislator. Lizzie Eustace could endow
him : but he gets little pleasure from life, poor man, as he
approaches nearer and nearer to betrayal of Lucy by his
intimacy with the predatory Lizzie. His inner freedom and
his outer manner are constrained by his disgust—not only
with Lady Eustace but with himself. Not till he returns
to Lucy are the doors of his heart reopened and he can relax
again. (One wonders, incidentally, what Trollope would
have done for a plot in this and several other cases, if the
Act for payment of M.P.s had been passed in his lifetime :
Greystock, Phineas Finn, George Vavasour and others would
not have had to let the advantages of a rich wife weigh so
heavily with them if they could have combined patriotism
with breadwinning.)

Lopez of *The Prime Minister* and Melmotte of *The Way We Live Now* sink beneath the conflict between lust for wealth and social position and their submerged yearning for respect : they die miserably, half recognising their failure. Lady Glencora in *Can You Forgive Her ?* is torn between adolescent passion and a pathetic desire to be " good "—a real longing to love a husband who makes tender love impossible until her threatened elopement breaks down his remoteness. Louis Trevelyan in *He Knew He Was Right,* sacrifices his sanity to the obstinacy which will not allow him to admit his wife's innocence. (This story is an interesting example of a case where Trollope's direct vision acted against his conventional judgment : he himself believed the book to be a failure because, having drawn an accurate picture of a neurotic who ruins his own and his wife's lives, he could not contrive to attract sympathy for him : the reader can only hope for the dissolution of the marriage, and this, of course, was not a hope which Trollope cared to encourage.) In the same story, Nora Rowley, recognises the pull between position, as represented by a gallant young nobleman, and love, as represented by a poor but engaging journalist. She wavers as far as the drawing-room door behind which the earl's son will propose to her : but although the tug of war causes her to burst into tears when she rejects him, she remains firm and suffers considerable inconvenience, but no qualms, throughout the rest of the book. Phineas Finn, apart from his difficult decision about love, has to make political decisions which affect his integrity. He believes that he will act more honestly by following his admired leader and voting against the government whose servant he is. He wrecks his career (at least until the sequel) but one is left in doubt as to whether the conflict is quite as real as Phineas supposed. Trollope had no use for political dishonesty, but he also was well aware of the tendency of young men to make gestures to their own sense of drama. He poses another question implicitly in *Phineas Finn* : should a young statesman take his convictions at second hand ?

Although this theme of inward conflict and its resolution recurs so often that one can justifiably consider it predominant in Trollope's novels, there are several books in which he approaches the problem of living from other angles. The main plot of *The Last Chronicle*, for instance, concerns an upright and embittered man humiliated by a false charge of theft : Josiah Crawley, the perpetual curate of Hogglestock, does not fight with himself but with the world—though here again he is handicapped in the fight by the limitations of his nature, his pride, harshness and lack of charity. The craggy, magnificent story of Crawley is linked to two others : the story of Henry Grantly's wooing of Josiah's daughter, Grace, who, though softer and less spirited than Lucy Robarts, like her will not surrender to her lover till she is sure that she can be received as an equal by Grantly's family ; and the agonised, almost inarticulate conflict between Archdeacon Grantly and his son centring around his son's love for Grace. Looked at from one angle this book might be considered a witty and subtle study of pride. There is Crawley's pride, which allows him brutally to reject friendship and to allow his wife and children to starve rather than to accept the most delicately offered help (Trollope excels at describing degrees of delicacy in behaviour) ; pride in his own merit and scholarship which causes him to eat out his heart in bitterness at the thought of others, less scholarly than he, succeeding in a world he despises. There is the gentle pride of Grace Crawley ; there is the worldly pride

of the Archdeacon. Agonised and consumed by their prides
—and quite unconscious of them—the characters work
their way through the crises which block the flow of their
personalities and win through to those serene final chapters
where the perpetual curate, forced into a new coat by his
wife, is at last induced to sit down to dinner with the
Archdeacon.

*The Last Chronicle* is one of Trollope's greatest books
(his own judgment and ours meet on this) and from the point
of view of construction a remarkable achievement. For
apart from the Barsetshire stories of the Crawleys and
Grantlys, we get also the end of the story of Lily Dale,
Adolphus Crosbie and Johnny Eames—her final rejection
of both lovers—and the delicious adventures of Johnny
Eames and his friend Conway Dalrymple the artist, among
the middle class of Bayswater. Never has that world and
its circumstances been so subtly drawn or with so little
exaggeration or bitterness as Trollope drew it in the
Broughton sequence in this book—its ineffectiveness, its
snobbery, its false values, its atmosphere of stale port in the
dining-room, the unreal and pretentious romanticism of
its women. It is purest comedy, never coarsened by
caricature. Remote as are the Bayswater scenes and the
scenes in Sir Raffle Buffle's office, where Johnny Eames
behaves with such impudence, from Barsetshire, however,
the texture of the book is so closely woven that it suffers
no breaks or stoppages. Almost any book read immediately
after *The Last Chronicle* (except some of Trollope's own)
seems insubstantial or laboured, lacking thickness and
variety of life.

This same thickness is found in *The Way We Live Now*,
where the inner conflict is again less important—or more

deeply hidden—than is the dominating theme : the decay
of society which sets in when aristocracy sells its honour for
wealth. Here too are five distinct stories besides other inter-
weavings among the characters which almost amount to
plots. Like *The Last Chronicle* and *The Prime Minister,*
the book as a whole attains an eminence which is reached
only here and there in Trollope's lesser books. It is a giant
among Victorian novels, though, oddly enough, it is seldom
read now and Trollope himself did not altogether approve
of it. His own opinion of it is worth quoting since it shows
not only the extent to which the book may be taken as a true
picture of the times, but also his own uneasiness about the
way the world was going. (It is from these notes, in his
Autobiography, that the passage on Carlyle and the other
prophets of the age were quoted earlier.)

I began a novel, to the writing of which I was instigated by
what I conceived to be the commercial profligacy of the age.
Whether the world does or does not become more wicked as
the years go on, is a question which probably has disturbed the
minds of thinkers since the world began to think. That men
have become less cruel, less violent, less selfish, less brutal,
there can be no doubt ; but have they become less honest ?
[Then follows the passage quoted on p. 30]. Nevertheless a
certain class of dishonesty, dishonesty magnificent in its pro-
portions, and climbing into high places, has become at the
same time so rampant and so splendid that there seems to be
reason for fearing that men and women will be taught to feel
that dishonesty, if it can become splendid, will cease to be
abominable. . . . Instigated, I say, by some such reflections
as these, I sat down in my new house to write *The Way We
Live Now.* And as I had ventured to take the whip of the
satirist into my hand, I went beyond the iniquities of the
great speculator who robs everybody, and made an onslaught
also on other vices—on the intrigues of girls who want to get
married, on the luxury of young men who prefer to remain

single, and on the puffing propensities of authors who desire to cheat the public into buying their volumes.

The book has the fault which is to be attributed to almost all satires, whether in prose or verse. The accusations are exaggerated. . . . In other respects *The Way We Live Now* was, as a satire, powerful and good. The character of Melmotte is well maintained. The Bear-garden is amusing—and not untrue, the Longestaffe girls and their friend, Lady Monogram, are amusing—but exaggerated. Dolly Longestaffe, is, I think, very good. And Lady Carbury's literary efforts are, I am sorry to say, such as are too frequently made. But here again the young lady with her two lovers is weak and vapid. . . . The interest of the story lies among the wicked and foolish people.

In spite of Trollope's strictures upon his own exaggeration, *The Way We Live Now* is in fact a far less exaggerated satire than any which either Dickens or Thackeray produced ; its degree of sophistication, in this respect, is remarkable. Scoundrelly financiers have better manners to-day than had Melmotte, and the impoverished aristocrat is less gullible and less useless to society ; but otherwise—allowing for differences in conventions—the story to-day hardly strikes one as satire at all. (Perhaps this is a reflection on the honesty of our own times.) Apart from its satire, the book contains some magnificently dramatic scenes—Melmotte's speech in Parliament for instance—and one deeply moving one— the proposal of Lady Carbury's middle-aged suitor and her acceptance of him.

*The Way We Live Now* shares the sombre quality of *The Bertrams* though it is less romantic ; and the comprehensiveness of *The Prime Minister*, but without quite attaining the implicit nobility of that work.

In a few novels he dealt more particularly with a situation —*Orley Farm* is one of these, but the best is surely *The Eustace Diamonds*, a social thriller and a first-rate story of a thoroughly unpleasant adventuress who is redeemed only by a certain dash and courage which Trollope only allows himself to approve of when she is in the hunting field. The story is taut with suspense—" will she pull it off this time ? "—and lit all through with exquisite comedy. It is full of movement—real screen play—ranging over the innocent home-life of Lady Fawn's household in Richmond, the gay comings and goings of Mayfair, Lady Linlithgow's dreary ménage in Bruton Street, Lizzie Eustace's seaside castle in Scotland, the smutty interiors of trains, government offices. Back and forth we go among them all, pursuing Lizzie and her diamonds, hastening in the wake of semi-reluctant lovers, catching up with the gossip, meeting briefly with old friends from other books. The story concludes with a perfect Trollope finish : a house-party at the Duke of Omnium's delightedly bring to an end an evening devoted to gossip about Lady Eustace :

" I call that woman a perfect godsend. What should we have done without her ? " This Lady Glencora said almost to herself as she prepared to join the duke. The duke had only one more observation to make before he retired for the night. " I'm afraid, you know, that your friend hasn't what I call a good time before her, Glencora." In this opinion of the Duke of Omnium's the readers of this story will perhaps agree.

## V

TROLLOPE'S genius for creating life lay, as one would expect with a man of his capacity for direct vision, in dialogue and in the objective setting down of movement and scene. Using these in combination, he achieved a high degree of emotional tension, of suspense or humour. One gets the feeling, sometimes, that while Trollope's pen was transcribing what he was "hearing" and "seeing" at the moment of writing, it was operating on a plane of reality which his conscious mind hardly apprehended. It appears often that his consciousness came into play after his unconscious had operated, and pulled his characters back to fit a place for which they had grown too large. This is more obviously the case where the moral value is at issue. Most readers of Trollope must have realised sadly that when a man exhibits gaiety, grace and intellect he is very likely to come to grief; Crosbie, Alaric Tudor, Ralph Newton (to a lesser degree) are all examples of what Lily Dale describes as "the Apollos of the world—the Apollos in heart who are so full of feeling, so soft-hearted, so kind, who never say a cross word" and who, she goes on, "it so often turns out . . . won't wash." Jane Austen, of course, treats her Crawfords in *Mansfield Park* with something of the same severity. This disapproval is a remnant on the part of both writers, perhaps, of the country town's middle-class suspicion of the goings on of metropolitanites. Yet each must have had a guilty enjoyment of wit, intellect and ease of manner—or how could they so aptly reproduce it?

The cinematographic subtlety of Trollope's scenes is an outstanding quality in his novels. As on the screen, the characters move continually among objects and within time, light and space, too, play on the reader's consciousness. Occasions where the scenes transcend the book as a whole are often to be found. It could be said that while by no means all Trollope's novels are first rate, there are practically no books which do not contain scenes of very great quality. His dialogue in itself shows a penetration into human psychology which some of his own animadversions on novel-writing tend to obscure. Take, for instance, these lines from *The Last Chronicle*, where Lily Dale explains to her mother why she will not take Crosbie back.

> " If it were simply myself and my own future fate in life, I would trust him with it to-morrow, without a word. I would go to him as a gambler goes to the gambling table, knowing that if I lost everything I could hardly be poorer than I was before. . . . That, however, is not my difficulty . . . I think so well of myself that loving him as I do—yes, Mamma, don't be uneasy, loving him as I do, I believe I could be a comfort to him . . . if he would teach himself to look back upon the past as I can do and to judge of me as I can judge of him."
>
> " He has nothing, at least, for which to condemn you."
>
> " But he would have, were I to marry him now. He would condemn me because I had forgiven him. He would condemn me because I had borne what he had done to me, and had still loved him. . . . He would recognise this after a while and would despise me for it. But he would not see what there is of devotion to him in my being able to bear the taunts of the world in going back to him, and your taunts and my own taunts."

It is wonderful to think that the man who wrote this praised the character of Thackeray's Amelia, as one which everyone would love, and for its likeness to nature !

Lily Dale is allowed her merit to the end—though Trollope did call her a " French prig " (whatever he meant by that).

Some of his women are not so fortunate : Winifred Hurtle, the passionate, tragic American in *The Way We Live Now*, a life-sized figure, capable of tenderness and truthfulness is left with a slur on her character in order that that weak-kneed young man, Paul Montague, can be partnered off with the *jeune fille* of the book. Mrs. Hurtle thought her husband had died, and apparently it has to be reckoned against her that she did not know he had failed to do so. Trollope failed to face up to something when he dared not make Mrs. Hurtle a noble woman simply because she was American and passionate. She is vindicated by Mrs. Max Goesler, that most delightful of heroines, the Viennese Jewess, sophisticated, courageous, civilised, who is allowed to marry Phineas Finn, even though, in a scene memorable in English fiction, she declares her love and even offers him money. On the other hand, the adorable Lady Glencora, honest and innocent in her spoken words, gentle as a child and sweet natured—as well, of course, as sardonic—must never forget that she nearly sinned ; the echoes of that youthful impulse are heard down the years, even into *The Duke's Children* when she is dead.

Oddly enough, this judgment of Trollope's against some of his most fully realised and attractive characters does not produce inconsistencies or faulty weighting, perhaps because one feels that the characters are greater than the things that happen to them—what Trollope's inward eye perceived was more real than what he consciously thought (or thought he thought). The comparison of the inward life of the characters with his moral " grading " of them is made here only to emphasise his supernormal faculties when he used, or was used by, his direct approach to the world. As he grew older this direct approach informed his writing more fully—or perhaps it is truer to say that his native wisdom added to his, by now, vast experience of living, was more receptive to what he apprehended and less cut off from his artist's vision by arbitrary conventional judgments. He is, at least, less arbitrary in his own implied judgments on the men and women of his later books ; their fates are more acceptable to us who champion them. We win, for instance, two notable victories : Mrs. Max Goesler is admitted to be a very great lady, although her background is as obscure as Melmotte's or the Rev. Emilius's, and, in a lesser book, Mary Lowther (in *The Vicar of Bullhampton*) is allowed to engage herself to Trollope's favourite type of good man, the country squire, to disengage herself with dignity and find happiness with a penniless soldier (not so penniless, it must be admitted, by the end of the book) who to our surprise and pleasure, remains a charming fellow although he is the " good " man's rival.

There are, of course, a multitude of characters—not all of them minor—who are allowed the full play of their characters uncramped by moral judgments. There are the series of enchanting, witty young women, of whom Violet Effingham, of *Phineas Finn,* is queen ; the magnificent old ladies ; Lady Lufton, so obstinate and yet so gracious ; the worried, motherly Lady Fawn, the frightening Lady Linithgow in her musty house, whom Lucy Morris companions in *The Eustace Diamonds.*

> When the wind is east or northeast, or even north, I am cross, for I have the lumbago. It's all very well talking about being good humoured. You can't be good humoured with the lumbago. And I have the gout sometimes in my knee. I'm cross enough then and so you'd be.

And dozens more : Trollope enjoyed old ladies. And quite
A.T.—5

as much as them he enjoyed, or rather, appreciated tall, pale, cold, young ladies who lived with their mothers on the edge of an inadequate income, counting on house-parties to see them through and wearily, disdainfully and repeatedly watching in ambush for a man who could support them in the style to which their mothers were accustomed ; Arabella, of *The American Senator*, Clara of *The Last Chronicle* and, less attractive because stupider, the de Courcy girls, the Longestaffe girls and the Gresham girls of several books.

Then in contrast, there are the dauntless, sardonic single women, some already resigned to spinsterdom, some braving themselves to accept it—Martha Dunstable (a real spinster even if she does marry Dr. Thorne in the end), Priscilla Stanbury, Miss Todd, Lily Dale (alas) and best of all, Lady Rosina de Courcy whom Plantagenet Palliser found so restful because she talked plainly about sensible concrete matters like cork soles.

He dealt with gusto with idiotic young men, " The Bear-garden " set, and with charming, inarticulate innocents like Silverbridge and Lord Gerald Palliser, to whom the Prime Minister was such a puzzled, anxious father (they took after their mother, Lady Glencora). He dealt tenderly if amusedly with the Americans, so concerned, so eager to understand our ways, so upright, so utterly puzzling to the casual unrational Englishmen they meet in the books ; the American Senator himself, the Boncassens of *The Duke's Children* (professorial, Bostonian) the Spaldings of *He Knew He Was Right* (diplomatic) and the rest, not forgetting Miss Wallachia Petrie, whose poem " Ancient Marbles While Ye Crumble " contained an occult and unfavourable reference to the British aristocracy. There are the ineffectives—of whom the most interesting is probably Sir Thomas

Underwood of *Ralph the Heir*, the gentle, eccentric, reserved old knight who not being able to endure the emotional pressures of family life, tucked his daughters away in a Fulham villa while he lived in the Temple, waiting for the day when he would feel like starting his Life of Bacon, and when at last his conscience pricked him into taking part in public life again, failing miserably in his election to Parliament. (In the story of this election Trollope recounts his own disheartening experience.) This is an unsurpassed study of the binding effects of accidie and of failure in responsibility.

Also there appears here and there in the books a significant figure variously disguised but fundamentally recognisable— the balanced, the orthodox man. It is a type of whom Trollope seems curiously fond and its recurrence in the books possibly throws some light on Trollope himself. We find this figure disguised now as Dr. Tempest in *The Last Chronicle*, now as the Rev. Mr. Puddicombe in *Dr. Wortle's School* ; we detect something of him in the Duke of St. Bungay and even in that most adult of characters, Josiah Monk of the Parliamentary novels. These men represent a worldly good sense ; against their cool impersonal judgments and their unfailing good manners is often set the impulsive, the sometimes indiscreet partisanship of the main character. These men would never have embroiled themselves with their colleagues or have shouted, as Trollope is said to have shouted in committee, " I differ from you entirely ! What was it you said ? "

No attempt can be made here to discuss comprehensively the variety of character and of characteristic which Trollope drew out of the world—even to have alluded to them in groups or types is misleading. His characters are indeed better read than read about. But there is in his books a recurring emphasis on the positive attitude to living and to feeling which is clearly seen in his main figures and which should not be overlooked. It is a marked characteristic of Trollope's " good " people that they say " yes " to a situation, and that having once tested themselves they cannot be put out of countenance ; they despise prevarication. Conversely, it is noticeable that many of his books are studies of uncertainty and dither in the central character. Uncertainty is their vice—an uncertainty that arises usually from lack of self-respect or self-knowledge. Phineas Finn dithers, in love and in politics ; Ralph the Heir dithers, Mark Robarts dithers, so does Paul Montague and so does Silverbridge—though the other young Lord, Lufton, does not. But oddly enough his women, even his heroines, seldom do. Clara Amedroz of *The Belton Estate*, an otherwise slightly colourless girl, takes on a noble reality when she openly declares herself to her worthless lover ; Mary Lowther, engaging herself under pressure to the wrong man, does so with heroic candour ; Winifred Hurtle confesses her love with admirable dignity and so does Mrs. Max Goesler. Violet Effingham both refuses and then accepts Chiltern's stormy addresses with a clean decision which reflects her single-mindedness. Even those who make a mistake do so with courage. It is, indeed, the women who are the heroic figures in Trollope's books on the whole (they are, too, noticeably more articulate than the men) ; the men who possess this, to Trollope, heroic quality, are nearly always minor characters—and this is, perhaps, why his minor characters are so prominent in our memories. The great exceptions to the uncertain hero are, of course, Plantagenet Palliser and Josiah Crawley. These, on the other hand, invite tragedy by their very inflexibility.

# VI

TROLLOPE'S sense of background was quite as penetrating as his knowledge of behaviour and his service with the Post Office gave him a familiarity with all of Southern England and with Ireland. He knew his market towns and country lanes, his Gatherum Castle and his " small old-fashioned brick house, abutting onto the road, but looking from its front windows onto a lawn and garden, which stretched down to the river." He knew the short cuts to Berkeley Square, his Mayfair, Bayswater and Pimlico (and just who lived there) ; he could exactly distinguish between Wiltshire villages, Somersetshire villages or the villages of the fen country.

He loved places and he had an exact sense of the importance of topography in fiction ; also he thoroughly understood the relation between architecture and social life. But what gives richness and depth to his scenes is his sensitiveness to the mood which immediate background and the time of day give to action. What happens, happens always in a particular place at a particular time of day or night. The noise of the running stream below the bridge on which he stands is forever part of our picture of Johnny Eames, as he faces the future without Lily ; the pitiless white Wiltshire road, under a morning sky, winds forever before Carrie Brattle as she desperately plods home ; Burgo Fitzgerald stands in the hall below and raises his hand as Lady Glencora mounts the stair and pauses to look down upon him ; Clara Amedroz waits for her lover to come down to dinner in the dark, chilly house where her aunt has just died ; the paper advertising the sale of his son's house flutters from the railings and the Archdeacon, sick at heart, spikes it off with his stick.

This sense of place and of objects (like the paper on the railings) is important in Trollope's creation of character : his people live and express themselves with things and in places ; high rooms and silence, or the bleak morning sunlight on dusty carpets, isolates them in their loneliness ; summer sunshine blesses young couples on picnics and river outings, or illumines the splendour of the great as they promenade the lawn at the Duchess of Omnium's garden party at Richmond.

It is Trollope's sense of scene that enables him to convey mobility—that mobility which gives a three-dimensional quality to his characters. They seek each other through a chain of ballrooms ; they wander through side doors into gardens ; meditating, they walk home across London from the House of Commons or the club ; they walk over the countryside, cross little bridges and wander down the side of ploughed fields. In his marvellous hunting scenes, the country flashes past at breakneck speed, the sky darkens and lightens overhead.

Trollope's art in using place and objects to intensify drama is seen at its height in the chapter of *The Prime Minister* entitled, simply, Tenway Junction. Lopez, the unscrupulous and heartless adventurer, has failed in all he set out to do ; he is now penniless, a charge on his contemptuous father-in-law, faced with disgrace and exile. One morning he kisses the wife he has so cruelly abused, tells her he has an appointment in Birmingham and leaves the house. Minutely, but without comment, Trollope tells how he takes the bus to Baker Street, the underground to Euston and there has

breakfast. Then he buys a first-class ticket to Tenway
Junction :

From this spot, some six or seven miles distant from London
lines diverge east, west, and north, north-east, and north-
west, round the metropolis in every direction, and with direct
communication with every other line in and out of London.
It is a marvellous place, quite unintelligible to the uninitiated,
and yet daily used by thousands who only know that when
they get there, they are to do what some one tells them. The
space occupied by the convergent rails seems to be sufficient
for a large farm. . . . Here and there and around there is
ever a wilderness of wagons, some loaded, some empty, some
smoking with close-packed oxen, and others furlongs in length
black with coals, which look as though they had been stranded
there by chance, and were never destined to get again into the
right path of traffic. Not a minute passes without a train going
here or there, some rushing by without noticing Tenway in
the least, crashing through like flashes of substantial lightning,
and others stopping, disgorging and taking up passengers by
the hundred. Men and women—especially the men, for the
women knowing their ignorance are generally willing to
trust to the pundits of the place—look doubtful, uneasy and
bewildered. But they all do get properly placed and unplaced,
so that the spectator at last acknowledges that over all this
apparent chaos there is presiding a great genius of order. From
dusky morn to dark night, and indeed almost throughout the
night, the air is loaded with a succession of shrieks. . . .
At Tenway Junction there are half-a-dozen long platforms
on which men and women and luggage are crowded. On
one of these for a while Ferdinand Lopez walked backwards
and forwards as though waiting for the coming of some especial
train. The crowd is ever so great that a man might be supposed
to walk there from morning to night without exciting special
notice. But the pundits are very clever, and have much experience in men and women. A well-taught pundit, who has
exercised authority for a year or two at such a station as that of
Tenway, will know within a minute of the appearance of each
stranger what is his purpose there . . . so that if his purport

be honest all necessary assistance may be rendered him. As Lopez was walking up and down, with smiling face and leisurely pace, now reading an advertisement and now watching the contortions of some amazed passenger, a certain pundit asked him his business. He was waiting, he said, for a train from Liverpool, intending, when his friend arrived, to go with him to Dulwich by a train which went round the west of London. It was all feasible, and the pundit told him that the stopping train from Liverpool was due there in six minutes, but that the express from the north would pass first. Lopez thanked the pundit and gave him sixpence—which made the pundit suspicious. A pundit hopes to be paid when he handles luggage, but has no such expectation when he merely gives information.

The pundit still had his eye on our friend when the shriek and the whirr of the express from the north was heard. Lopez walked quickly up towards the edge of the platform, when the pundit followed him, telling him that this was not his train. Lopez then ran a few yards along the platform, not noticing the man, reaching a spot that was unoccupied ; —and there he stood fixed. And as he stood the express flashed by. " I am fond of seeing them pass like that," said Lopez to the man who had followed him.

" But you shouldn't do it, sir," said the suspicious pundit. " No one isn't allowed to stand near like that. The very hair of it might take you off your legs when you're not used to it."

" All right, old fellow," said Lopez, retreating. The next train was the Liverpool train ; and it seemed that our friend's friend had not come, for when the Liverpool passengers had cleared themselves off, he was still walking up and down the platform. " He'll come by the next," said Lopez to the pundit, who now followed him about and kept an eye on him.

" There ain't another from Liverpool stopping here till the 2.20," said the pundit. " You had better come again if you mean to meet him by that."

" He has come on part of the way, and will reach this by some other train," said Lopez.

" There ain't nothing he can come by," said the pundit. " Gentlemen can't wait here all day, sir. The horders is against waiting on the platform."

" All right," said Lopez, moving away as though to make his exit through the station.

Now Tenway Junction is so big a place, and so scattered, that it is impossible that all the pundits should by any combined activity maintain to the letter that order of which our special pundit had spoken. Lopez, departing from the platform which he had hitherto occupied, was soon to be seen on another, walking up and down, and again waiting. But the old pundit had had his eye upon him, and had followed him round. At that moment there came a shriek louder than all the other shrieks, and the morning express down from Euston to Inverness was seen coming round the curve at a thousand miles an hour. Lopez turned round and looked at it, and again walked towards the edge of the platform. But now it was not exactly the edge that he neared, but a descent to a pathway—an inclined plane leading down to the level of the rails, and made there for certain purposes of traffic. As he did so the pundit called to him, and then made a rush at him—for our friend's back was turned to the coming train. But Lopez heeded not the call, and the rush was too late. With quick, but still with gentle and apparently unhurried steps, he walked down before the flying engine—and in a moment had been knocked into bloody atoms.

## VII

AS a novel-writer, Trollope's principal powers lay in his capacity to entertain, his sense of construction, his subtlety in drawing character, his almost un-rivalled capacity for drama (it was not for nothing that he attempted a play early in his career). But there is another quality in his work which gives it a stature not attained by many writers who can equal or even surpass him in craftsmanship. This quality can be described as maturity of outlook—" adultness " is really a closer definition. He had an all-around view of the world, seeing things, as it were, from the centre ; he had an adult concern for and with the activities which exercise adult minds. It is this sense of the importance of human activity which, in the last analysis, makes Anthony Trollope's writings non-trivial ; it is this which takes him out of the class of first-rate comedy-of-manners writers and which gives him a place of his own among Victorian novelists. It accounts of course, to a large extent, for his capacity to deal accurately with so many different professions and types, and for his being able to pass shrewd judgments on the state of affairs in places as foreign to his background as South Africa or the West Indies after his visits there. This adult " on-centre " quality of his enhanced, or was enhanced by, his direct vision and it accounted, too, for his dislike of distortion—his dislike, in other words, of letting a part grow out of proportion to a whole. It informs nearly every book of his. There are exceptions like *The Fixed Period* and *Brown, Jones and Robinson*. But it is in the parliamentary novels and in the sections of his books dealing with public life—with politics or the Civil Service—that it is most obviously displayed and it is from these that one can learn most fully to appreciate his work and his personality.

Men's work—what men do in creating and sustaining the civilisation in which they live—seemed to Trollope to be a matter of major interest. The interpretation of human nature, the line of the behaviour pattern, in work and in the relationships growing out of work, was to him as significant as behaviour in love or in any other private crisis. Of all work, he found himself most interested in the work which builds or maintains a nation—that is, in politics and public service. Trollope, it might be claimed, is perhaps the only English novelist who handles situations centring around both domestic and public life with equal subtlety, humour, pathos and sense of drama. In *Can You Forgive Her ?*, a deeply moving scene between Plantagenet Palliser and his wife Glencora, in which she tells him she has failed to love him, is followed by a scene in which he rejects high government office—the apex of his ambition. There is no drop in tension in the political scene, nor is it handled with any less subtlety and restraint than is the domestic scene preceding it. To Trollope the full capacity of man's nature could not be expressed in intimate relationships alone ; the serious novelist dealing with things as they are must exhibit personality exercising itself in the world outside as well.

Trollope's only serious rival in the field of the political novel of the period was Disraeli—a writer whom, as might be expected, he misunderstood and disliked. (" The wit has been the wit of hairdressers and the enterprise has been the enterprise of mountebanks "—so he writes of Disraeli's novels in the Autobiography.) Disraeli's *Endymion* was

written a few years after Trollope's *Phineas Finn*, and like
it, deals with the rise of a young politician—a rise con-
siderably helped by politically minded ladies. The attitude
of the two novelists towards the novel in general and this
subject in particular, is so completely opposed that it is
difficult even to compare them. Disraeli is a political theorist,
dealing with political ideas on the epic scale and his characters
are beyond life scale to match. Described with a formal
and scrupulous deliberation, they are set to perform their
functions, to carry their historical weight, and speak their
appropriate pieces. Though Disraeli depicts the ebb and
flow, the manoeuvrings and the strategies of political life,
the scale is far greater than in Trollope's novels—the scale
is of history, not of men's lives. With Disraeli, politics
are larger than life, with Trollope they are no larger than
life allows.

Disraeli thus describes his hero on the occasion of his
maiden speech.

> Endymion knew that this was the crisis of his life. He
> knew the subject well and he had all the tact and experience of
> Lord Roehampton to guide him. . . . Endymion slept very
> little that week, and the night before his motion not a wink.
> He almost wished he was dead as he walked down to the House
> in the hope that exercise might remedy or improve his languid
> circulation ; but in vain, and when his name was called and he
> had to rise, his hands and feet were like ice. . . . It might be
> said that he was sustained by his utter despair. He had a kind
> audience and an interested one. When he opened his mouth
> he forgot his first sentence, which he had long prepared. In
> trying to recall it and failing, he was for a moment confused.
> But it was only for a moment ; the unpremeditated came
> to his aid, and his voice, at first tremulous, was recognised as
> distinct and rich. There was a murmur of sympathy, and not
> merely from his own side. Suddenly, both physically and

intellectually he was quite himself. His arrested circulation flowed, and fed his stagnant brain. His statement was lucid, his arguments were difficult to encounter, and his manner modest. He sat down amid general applause and though he was then conscious that he had omitted more than one point on which he had relied, he was on the whole satisfied.

Here is Trollope's Phineas in the same situation.

The thing was now to be done. There he was with the House of Commons at his feet—a crowded House, bound to be his auditors as long as he should think fit to address them. . . . Phineas Finn had sundry gifts, a powerful and pleasant voice, which he had learned to modulate, a handsome presence and a certain natural mixture of modesty and self-reliance . . . and he had also the great advantage of friends in the House who were anxious that he should do well. But he had not that gift of slow blood . . . which would now have placed all his own resources within his own reach. . . . He became painfully conscious that he was repeating his own words. He was cheered almost from the outset, and yet he knew as he went on that he was failing. . . . He was going on with one platitude after another as to the benefit of reform . . . he pressed on fearing that words would fail him altogether if he paused ; but he did in truth speak very much too fast, knocking his words together. . . . But he had nothing to say for the bill except what hundreds had said before. As he became more and more conscious of his failure there grew upon him the idea—the dangerous hope that he might still save himself from ignominy by the eloquence of his invective. . . . He tried it and succeeded thoroughly in making the House understand that he was very angry, but he succeeded in nothing else. . . . Then he attempted to tell the story of Mr. Bunce in a light and airy way, failed and sat down in the middle of it. Again he was cheered by all around—cheered as a new member is usually cheered—and in the midst of the cheer would have blown out his brain had there been a pistol there for such an operation.

Here too is the experienced statesman in *Endymion*, speaking to the young man who admires him.

> Political trouble in this country never frightens me. Insurrection and riots strengthen an English government : they gave a new lease of life even to Lord Liverpool when his ministry was most feeble and unpopular : but economical discontent is quite another thing. The moment sedition arises from taxation, or want of employment, it is more dangerous and more difficult to deal with in this country than any other.

Trollope's minister, Monk, unburdens himself in very different tones.

> " I believe I did right to accept office. . . . Indeed unless a man does so when the bonds of office tendered to him are made compatible with his own views, he declines to proceed on the open path towards the prosecution of those views. A man who is combating one Ministry after another, and striving to imbue those Ministers with his own convictions, can hardly decline to become a Minister himself when he finds that those convictions of his own are henceforth . . to be the ministerial convictions of the day. . . . But let me tell you that the delight of political life is altogether in opposition . . . the very inaccuracy which is permitted to opposition is in itself a charm worth more than all the patronage and all the prestige of ministerial power. You'll try them both and then say if you do not agree with me. . . . That is all over now. They have got me into harness and my shoulders are sore. The oats, however, are of the best, and the hay is unexceptionable."

Trollope understood that a nation's political life is built up by men like other men—men who have wives at home and owe bills to their tailors. His parliamentary and Civil Service novels are therefore the stories of men working in politics, less than accounts of how politics work on men.

He had, indeed, considerable scepticism about political movements and about party legislation. As a man or a writer he was at the opposite end of the pole from Arnold, but his enchanting mockery of legislative bodies such as the Parliamentary Committee in *The Three Clerks* might have been written to accompany Arnold's sardonic remarks in *Friendship's Garland*. "To accustom oneself to regard the Marylebone Vestry, . . . or the Irish Church establishment, or our railways management . . . as absurdities—that is, I am sure, invaluable exercise for us just at present." But in spite of Trollope's mockery—mockery often so delicate that it is scarcely discernable ; which shows itself simply in meticulous reproduction—the impulse which makes men desire to devote themselves to legislation or to public service seemed to him to be a right, even a noble one. It represented, perhaps, to him the idea of *participation* and to the extrovert that he was, participation was the human duty of man. To put all one's effort however vainly into action which one believed to be relevant to the well-being of one's country, was in itself for him a good and right thing. In *Can You Forgive Her?*, again, there is a page or two devoted to a member who is called on by the Speaker at the end of a long day. As soon as he rises the members begin to stream out of the House. "He knew that he had worked for weeks and months to get up his facts and he was beginning to know that he had worked in vain . . . he had given heart and soul to this affair." The poor old lord is counted out before he finishes ; it is an unimportant little scene, good for two amusing pages. But there is something about the way Trollope describes it which recalls the reverence of *The Grammarian's Funeral,* the poem of Trollope's friend Browning.

In a passage just preceding this one Trollope allows himself to speak of what Parliament meant to him, without reserve or mockery.

> " I have told myself, in anger and in grief, that to die and not to have won that right of way, though but for a session . . . is to die and not to have done that which it most becomes an Englishman to have achieved. There are doubtless some who come out by that road, the loss of whose society is not to be regretted. England does not choose her six hundred and fifty-four best men. . . . Dishonesty, ignorance and vulgarity do not close the gate of that heaven against aspirants. . . . But . . . the best of her commoners do find their way there. It is the highest and most legitimate pride of an Englishman to have the letters M.P. written after his name."

Trollope was not personally particularly interested in causes or in party platforms. He was himself a Whig and later a Liberal but his political beliefs have a rather inconclusive fuzzy look to us to-day. He believed in " progress," but progress with a good brake on the wheels, which—he was relieved to see—would always be supplied by the Tory party. But it was immensely important to him that he was politically minded and he was " anxious that many who know aught of me should know " his political theory, which was the " continual diminution " of the distances between men in a " tendency towards equality," and without " sudden disruption of society." His views on political thinking are summed up in a lecture he gave to his Civil Service colleagues. " I would fain hope that every man in this service is a politician. I do not much mind what a man's politics are, so that he has got politics. So that he will concern himself with the public welfare of his country and of his race, and give his mind to the matter, I do not care whether I be called upon to agree with him, or to differ from him. But I do not love a man . . . who will say that politics are nothing to him. Such a one seems to me to shirk the first of a man's duties." Trollope, in fact, did not have a teleological view of politics, he was simply interested in the measurable benefit to be gained from any given piece of legislation and the degree of honesty which inspired it. What he understood so well about political life was the play of character on events, the strategy and manoeuvring, the use and ill-use of men by their commanding officers, the growth of responsibility and steadiness in the good men, the undermining effect of power on the weak and corruptible. With as much care and delight as he built up the structure of a love affair, with its sudden advances, its checks, its false trails, its unspoken communications, so he pictured the building up and the progress of a Government. In *The Prime Minister*, two stories run side by side, the story of Lopez, the social adventurer who marries a rich wife, as he believes, and ruins himself and her, and the story of Plantagenet Palliser's Coalition Government. Lopez's rise and fall, his dealings with the city, his fight for a seat in Parliament, his degrading treatment of his wife, is no less exciting than the struggle of Palliser to keep his cabinet together, the gradual disaffection of Sir Orlando Drought, the stupid man who can bring about the fall of a Government simply because he cannot be ignored, the growing grumbles in the House, the interplay between a serious and incorruptible premier and the opportunists, both honest and dishonest, who see trouble ahead.

In *Phineas Finn* the political interest is even more concentrated ; it is the story of the political growth of a young man's mind from the moment he takes his seat to the point where, having held a minor post in the Government, he

A.T.—6

resigns because he cannot vote with his party on an Irish measure. His return to politics and eventual success is described in *Phineas Redux* and in *The Prime Minister*. It is here that we see Trollope using politics as material for living ; *Phineas Finn* is a kind of *Pilgrim's Progress,* if a novel so sophisticated and objective as this can be paralleled to that simple allegory. Phineas grows up under the compulsions of that most grown-up of professions, politics. The obstinacy, pride, weakness and ambition of men interweave and balance the strength, honesty, quickness and devotion of others. He learns how the shifting of opinion through a whisper or a silence, may be used to disturb the perfect balance which keeps a government steady in its progress ; how to time speeches so that they carry a weight which does not derive only from their content. He learns how dangerous men can be used and how good men can fail. He learns in fact the " know how " of political life, which is no more than the " know how " of any professional life but which is more essential to success in politics than to success in other professions. It was indeed this " know how " that so much interested Trollope : and it is possible that he delighted in politics largely because they demanded a kind of expertise in conduct which only really adult and experienced men can provide. And though it is true that Trollope had a tenderness for the gangling, the Johnny Eameses and the Charley Tudors—gauche, unsophisticated and innocent—no one can read his more mature works without divining that the men he admired were those who had learnt the ways of the world without becoming too embittered and without suffering corruption, but who had, nevertheless acquired an ironic patience with the world. His saints, Plantagenet Palliser on the one hand or Mr.

Harding on the other, he loved and revered, but his chosen companion, the man he felt for with all his soul was pretty certainly Phineas's mentor, Josiah Monk.

" Mr. Monk," said Phineas [who has just made his maiden speech], " I have made an ass of myself so thoroughly that there will at any rate be this good result, that I shall never make an ass of myself again after that fashion."

" Ah ! " [replies Monk, who has followed him in his despairing exit from the House that night] " I thought you had some such feeling as that, and therefore I was determined to speak to you. You may be sure Finn, that I do not care to flatter you, and I think you ought to know that, as far as I am able, I will tell you the truth. Your speech, which was certainly nothing great, was about on a par with other maiden speeches in the House of Commons. You have done yourself neither good nor harm. Nor was it desirable that you should. My advice to you now is, never to avoid speaking on any subject that interests you, but never to speak for above three minutes till you find yourself as much at home on your legs as you are now when sitting. But do not suppose that you have made an ass of yourself—that is, in any special degree."

So long as England is " governed by committee," so long, that is, that the toughness or pliability, quickwittedness or doggedness, veniality or honesty of individuals is called into play in legislation, and so long as timing, patience and judgment can be effectively used in promoting legislation, so long will Trollope's parliamentary novels be found apposite and illuminating. The imaginary, but quite plausible Acts on which he hangs his political action are of course of only historical interest ; his general political observations (like his amused comment that no party which comes to power ever wishes seriously to reverse the machine and travel in the other direction ; no party, for instance, has any revolutionary aim) are out of date. But it is not with these matters that he is deeply concerned, but with method and men. Although Trollope's statesmen are unidentifiable (though some rather far-fetched likenesses have been deduced) and his legislation imaginary, his political novels throw a light on contemporary political thought which is extremely illuminating for the amateur historian. We get a good view of the Reform Bills in action—for we see young reformers unseated by them. We get a good view, from the uneasy Whig benches, of the obstreperous new Radicals from the north. Most interesting of all we look, as consciously as Trollope looked, on a political world where the prestige of old blood and broad acres was giving way to new powers unleashed by a widened franchise on the one hand and by the rising influence of industrial wealth on the other. Phineas Finn accepts a seat which is (for all the abolition of pocket boroughs) still recognised as being in the gift of the Earl of Brentford. Only a few years later the new Duke of Omnium (Plantagenet Palliser of the earlier books) refuses to lend his name to back any candidate at all for the local constituency—although his wife considers this to be fatuously quixotic behaviour. One of the most fascinating passages of *The Prime Minister* consists of a conversation between the new Duke of Omnium and the old Duke of St. Bungay—whose Cabinet days dated back to the time of the Duke of Wellington—on the disposal of a Garter. The young Duke believes that it should be conferred for merit, irrespective of party allegiance or prestige ; he proposes to give it to an obscure old Earl who never opened his mouth in Parliament but had devoted himself to the improvement of the labouring classes. The old Duke is profoundly shocked by the suggestion. In his view the Garter is conferred as an appropriate honour on those whose position in the country—by virtue of their rank, wealth and prestige—entitles them to carry so high a decoration. The young Duke persists in his opinion. It is a scene which sums up the break in political and social tradition which occurred after the first Reform Bill.

It is characteristic of Trollope that he should understand as clearly as he did the forces which motivated English political life in his time, the impulses and restraints which can be found in English political life at any time, and yet when desirous of setting down a political credo of his own, should have fallen into such timid and inconclusive language. It is again a matter of direct vision versus cerebration. His artist's eye gave him, in politics, as in other fields of living, a picture whose truth was often beyond the grasp of his critical faculties.

## VIII

IT has been suggested here that Trollope's central view of life gave his writing a wholeness, a sort of compre-hensiveness, which is perhaps his distinguishing quality as a novelist. He stands at the centre of his world—a world comprising not only people but nature and objects—and he observes and understands the operation of people on each other and of objects and time and movement and seasons upon people. His direct vision, when he allowed it full play, enabled him to receive emanations of personality and of feeling which usually pass unnoticed except by writers who are concerned mainly with the psychological approach. He lacked, indeed, what he called " transcendentalism " ; though he stood at the centre of the world he did not rise above it, and an itch for wings worried him at times. But if he could not rise free of his world, he did to some extent rise free of his time. Most writers of his age—the writers who were active up to the 'eighties—were men of their time and to some degree pushed around by their time. Trollope, for all his prejudices, was less shackled than most of his contemporary fellow-novelists.

Trollope's comprehensiveness of view and his lack of desire to " score off " the world, which is related to this comprehensiveness, is the more remarkable because his childhood and youth were so particularly unhappy. The unhappiness rose not so much from actual ill-treatment (though he had a good deal of that at school) as from those things which most tend to cripple and sour a man—shame, poverty, humiliation, loneliness. He had every excuse for a grudge against the world and he had in his writing a means of putting the grudge to good use. How little he was the victim of the complexes and inhibitions we should now expect to find in a man with that childhood, one can see from his Autobiography. For him, life seems to have renewed itself daily ; he would not allow himself to be a victim to what had passed ; the living present claimed him and he wholeheartedly went out to meet it. So he absorbed experience, which hurt him often enough, but which never poisoned him. He was in a curious way a released soul, released from his time, from his own past and from his own books. Though he lived with his books—or with the characters in them—as he describes in his Autobiography, he was not tied into them ; the writing of them was not, that is to say, essential to his own spiritual wholeness. He wrote for money ; he wrote as often as anyone offered him any money to do so and he loved to write. He wanted to be famous. But he did not have to express himself in writing ; he expressed himself in life. Writing for money as he did (or for fame, or for occupation) he was released from the awful need to justify himself in his work. He did not need to cut up his own soul ; all he had to do was to open the door of his mind on to the world and let the world flow in, unobstructed. No anguish laid him low ; he merely created.

Trollope's personal life may not have greatly affected his powers as a writer (except in so far as it provided him with copy). He was perhaps unusual among writers in this. We have rather to thank his direct vision and his receptive powers for his achievement as a novelist, but his professional life undoubtedly enhanced his clarity of vision and helped to develop his almost unrivalled sense of proportion, his particular " grown up " quality and his " on centre " point of view. Trollope was a Civil Servant.

The Civil Service has altered a good deal from the time Trollope entered it (though when he left it, the first of the reforms which built up the modern Service had been put into practice), but then as now the Civil Servant had a kind of detached independence of spirit which came from the consciousness of being an employee of the nation. Lily Dale sympathises with Johnny Eames because he has to serve so crotchety a superior officer as Sir Raffle Buffle. " I don't serve him. I serve the Queen—or rather the public " retorts Johnny. The Civil Servant, too, either because of the nature of his work or because he lives in a professionally homogeneous world, has a peculiar capacity for immersing himself in his job and becoming (at least in the case of the intelligent worker) profoundly interested in its purpose. To senior Civil Servants at least, their work seems to be above all things urgent and important. Trollope says simply, " I became intensely anxious that people should have their letters delivered to them punctually," and this feeling of the significance and reality of his job—of the whole job of national administration—was probably largely responsible for Trollope's sense of a world operating outside of himself and for his preoccupation with adult interests in his books. He had never written a book till he had served in the Post Office for some years ; he had only scribbled down his day-dreams. His administrative job in the Post Office removed his centre from himself and so freed him from the claustro-phobia of introspection which has suffocated or ruined many would-be writers.

Not only did his work free him from egocentricity, but it obliged him, by its very nature, to regard the world and

the individuals who compose it, objectively.  His business
was concerned with the working of a service that touched
society through its individual members : Trollope had to
learn how to assess the weight and the validity of claims,
complaints and misunderstandings, he had to understand
the functioning of professions and of businesses : the delivery
of mails is a matter very intimately tied up with living.
Any Civil Servant must understand the needs and difficulties
of all grades of society and regard the individuals who
compose them without the prejudices or associations which
are inherent in a purely social, political or even artistic
approach.  This detachment gives clarity (and, often, charity)
to the point of view and this clarity too is enhanced often
by the official's need for conscientiousness and accuracy
in reporting.  Trollope's extraordinary perception of the
working of society and of its gradations must have owed
a good deal to his official training—though it is also obvious
that his own directness of vision and his honesty helped to
make him the extremely able Civil Servant that he was.

Another thing which the Service did for Trollope (as
for many others who enter it) was to give him a conviction
of national progress—a slow certain progress—and this
conviction tempered intolerance.  (By the same token,
it made him, however, somewhat impatient of the Press, with
its sometimes mistimed eagerness to " expose "—an impatience shared by most of his colleagues, then and now.)
Trollope, like his colleagues, worked (metaphorically) at
the centre of things—in, as it were, the legislative workshop.
He could see legislation being built up, piece by piece ; he,
like his colleagues, could see at close range the daily approaches
made to remedy injustice, to enlarge and develop the capacity
of law and custom to create a wider equality, to eliminate

the barriers to the daily ease of living ; to avoid the false trails which lead to impingement of liberties in the long run. Like all responsible Civil Servants, he watched, and indeed sometimes initiated the first steps in these approaches, knowing how long the path must be which leads from the first memorandum to the last supplementary question after the Act is passed and in operation. Like them he knew how the man in the government office must circle and circumvent —dodge this man's prejudices and that man's venality, take shelter (covering his beloved scheme from assault) while the uninformed and the professional objector either called down wrath from heaven on delays or attacked a purpose they did not understand. He had to learn the Civil Service lesson—to feel no partisanship in all of this ; to show no sense of alliance with those in public life who backed his colleagues' efforts and no disdain or impatience with those who libelled them : to show no pleasure at success, to claim no part in success, and no chagrin at failure, though he must often shoulder the blame for an undertaking which he had in fact advised against. But his reward—the reward of the Service—was that he lived and worked with the sense that he was seeing built up around him, and sometimes, with his own help, a vast structure. Acts of Parliament, Orders in Council, Statutory Rules and Orders—those abstractions so aridly dull to the public—were to him the joists and beams of a nation's destiny, and he could know that even the small internal businesses—the minutes, the reports, the " chits " played an important part in the structure, though they were invisible to the public eye.

Knowing that the work of building this structure was continuing every day, that each file that passed over a desk contributed in some way towards it, a man in the Civil

Service can have a far greater awareness of the certainty of progress than of the importance of anomalies. The anomalies are topical and will in time be dealt with ; but the principle of continued improvement which causes the anomaly to be that only, and not, in fact, an accepted evil, is eternal.

This point of view had a profound influence on Trollope and one might say was responsible to a large extent for his detachment—for his, to some, possibly too great detachment—from social evils. It was almost certainly partly responsible for his lack of sympathy with what he called " Carlyleism."

Trollope, who made a good deal of trouble in his branch of the Service, being, like many intelligent officials, a rebel, a positive Hampden for his own and his colleagues' rights and at the same time, like many officials, profoundly mistrustful of internal changes in the Service, particularly when suggested by those outside it, was nevertheless an extremely able Civil Servant. Though he bogged down badly at the start, when he was a lowly copyist, he rose very high, so high that he was at the end a candidate for the Under-secretaryship (losing the job, probably, simply on account of his rampageous personality). For all his " banging about " (as Froude described it), and his rows with his superiors, he loved the Service and understood it. In a lecture which caused some fury in the upper circles of the Service and in which Trollope was protesting against the proposals to award promotion on merit instead of on seniority and competence, he says, " there is no profession by which a man can earn his bread in these realms, admitting of a brighter honesty, of a nobler purpose or of an action more manly and independent." The protest and the tribute are typical both of his loyalty and his conservatism. The Post

Office, of which he was an official, was a branch of the Service particularly well suited to him ; he became a Deputy Surveyor while fairly young (for he was willing, in his unhappiness in London, to take an Irish post as Surveyor's clerk, which no one else cared to do and which quickly led to his promotion), and rose to be a Surveyor. This entailed his roving all over the region allotted to him, looking into the Post Office establishments, investigating the deliveries and generally improving and cleaning up the machinery of communications. He could work as he liked and his recommendations could rarely be gainsaid. A Surveyor was more or less a monarch in his own field and this suited Trollope very well ; moreover, a Surveyor was in the very enviable position of being able to see his recommendations put into operation, and this was highly stimulating to a conscientious worker like Trollope. Surveyors, in fact, tended to be, or to become, a special race of men (the office was abolished only a few years ago). They often were, as individuals, markedly of the Trollope type—lusty, enthusiastic, outspoken, filled with fervour for their job and, like Trollope, apt to plunge wholeheartedly into the rural pursuits of their region. Trollope describes how he hunted with whatever pack he found in the district, and how he often amazed cottage-dwellers by bursting, booted and habited, into their homes to ask about their postal deliveries. Apart from this routine work in England and Ireland Trollope was also entrusted with many important missions abroad : he negotiated postal agreements in Egypt and in the United States.

Trollope loved and honoured the Service for its integrity and its seriousness of purpose, but he also (again like most of his colleagues at all times) deeply relished the drama and intercourse of its world. He watched with interest the subtleties of relationships and the diversions which arise around an established hierarchy, and this understanding of the nuances of " above " and " below " which play so important a part in Civil Service life, sharpened his sense of hierarchy in the outer world, so that no writer can touch off the delicate distinctions between professions, incomes, places of residence, family connections and so forth, as he can. He knew, as all Civil Servants know, the extremity of the urge for promotion—the only reward given for labour —and the Civil Servant's weakness, the desire for power ; power, not as the world knows it, but power to have a chance to get more work into his hand, to know a bit more of the total picture, to understand more of what is going on in the upper air. He could see this urge operating in a small field, its repercussions on colleagues sitting at the next desk. He could see, in fact, the effect, at close range, of any man's personality on his neighbour. For in the Civil Service, men work under pressure not only of urgent instructions from above, but of the personality, pleasing or unpleasing, demanding or unselfish, of their very proximate colleagues ; personality is magnified by proximity to more than life size. He loved the struggle of wills—a struggle which can be carried on with a good deal of freedom within a public service (and he carried on his own duel with Rowland Hill, the Secretary, and an " outsider," during the greater part of his Post Office career). " How I loved," he remarks nostalgically in his Autobiography, " when I was contradicted—as I was very often and no doubt very properly—to do instantly as I was bid, and then to prove that what I was doing was fatuous, dishonest, expensive and impracticable ! And then there were feuds—such delicious feuds ! "

He was delighted by the comic element that must enter into official machinery and by the inflexible absurdity of the less-intelligent officials whose only quality was a kind of arid honesty, and who joyfully tied themselves up in red tape.

The Civil Service enters into a large number of Trollope's books—he cannot resist it; in *John Caldigate* he turns the plot on a bit of detective work by the most engaging of earnest, eager little clerks, Bagwax of the Post Office. Throughout the Barsetshires we have Johnny Eames alternately bullying and being bullied by his superior officer, Sir Raffle Buffle. But it is in *The Three Clerks* that he allowed himself full scope and it is significant that although this is a very early book, and although it does not have the power nor the comprehensiveness of, say, *The Prime Minister, Phineas Finn* or *The Way We Live Now* on the one hand, nor the piercing, almost bitter vision into human relations that can be found in what might be called his " psychological novels "—*He Knew He Was Right* or *John Caldigate*—yet as a study of conduct and day-to-day relations between people, professionally and socially, and of the conflict within men's natures, this book holds a place of its own among his works. With *Framley Parsonage,* and for quite different reasons, it seems to be particularly Trollope's personal statement. It is of course, partly autobiographical, but the biographical parts of the book are not more expressive of the writer than the others.

There is more to the story than the account of three clerks in two Government offices—it is a lyrical account of innocent young love, of courtship carried on in perhaps the most enchanting *mise en scène* that Trollope ever devised, the Thames-side cottage of Mrs. Woodward and her three daughters. To this cottage come the three young men at holiday weekends : the girls grow from little sisters to lovely young women, the rollicking afternoons spent punting between the islands become charged with deeper feeling, a tension which disturbs and even saddens them. Love ensues—not always happily—but the magic of that early sunshine happiness remains to brighten the book to the end. Trollope never achieved anything more tender and more delicately painted than the life at Surbiton Cottage.

But the other and the main concern of the book is with the clerks, two of them in the admirable, the model, Government Department, the Weights and Measures Office, and the third, Charley, in the most unexemplary office of Internal Navigation. It is for Charley's career in this office that Trollope drew so largely on his own early experiences but he drew on these simply for comic material and his general Civil Service observation goes more particularly into his account of the " Weights and Measures " and of the staff who worked there.

The background of the Government office gives him exactly what he needs for comedy and for creating suspense— for one of Trollope's particular talents lies in the power to create almost unbearable anxiety on the reader's part as to the outcome of minor day-to-day crises ; and the life of ambitious young clerks, in the Civil Service or any other profession, are full of day-to-day crises, absorbing to themselves, but, save when Trollope handles them, seldom very absorbing to others. The introduction of the first examinations for promotion, its repercussions on the friendship of the clerks, Alaric and Harry, the effect of these repercussions on their weekends at the cottage ; the degree of tact and imagination which must be exercised, not only

by the two rival friends, but by those that love them both,
when the unknown powers impose such a test upon ability
and character—from these things Trollope creates a drama
of human feeling and no one who follows it will question
that it is indeed substantial material for drama. It is from
small crises of this kind that the contours of a man's character
are moulded. The greater drama arising from this smaller
one, comes through the ambition of Alaric—so charming,
so witty and so able an official—who is inveigled by an
aristocratic younger son, of shabby morality, into specula-
tion and, unwillingly, into embezzlement. In the Hon.
Undy Scott, Trollope drew a complete cad—equalled only
by Sir Felix Carbury in *The Way We Live Now*, for pure
despicable behaviour—and he says what he thinks of him
with unusual bitterness. The moral betrayal of Alaric, whom
Trollope had to love, and whom the reader too must love,
represents the deliberate ruin by the worthless, the unpro-
fessional waster, of an integrity which was owed not only
to the victim's family, but to that service which, Trollope
believed, demanded the best that a man could give.

The book contains one of Trollope's best pieces of satiric
reportage—a Parliamentary committee in action, a piece
of comedy writing which could be isolated from the book
as a complete short work of humour. It contains a perfect
" official " of the kind which will survive as long as a Civil
Service exists anywhere, Mr. Fidus Neverbend, whose
knowledge of protocol and official forms availed him so
little when he had to put on miner's clothes and descend in
a miner's cage on an official investigation. " Indeed all his
air of command, all his personal dignity and dictatorial
tone, left him. . . . He was like a cock whose feathers had
been trailed through the mud and who could no longer

crow aloud. . . . His appearance was somewhat that of a dirty dissipated cook, who, having been turned out of one of the clubs for drunkenness had been wandering about the streets all night." It contains also a picture of shabby gentility which equals the Broughton sections of *The Last Chronicle*.

But what one finds to perfection in *The Three Clerks* is the Trollope " scene," the cinematographic account of an exchange between people at a moment in which the atmosphere is heavy with feeling and the relationships are tense with what is unspoken. In *The Three Clerks* there is one such scene, slight enough in itself and yet memorable among many others, because it is a notable example of Trollope's technique in using gesture and objects as well as speech, and of his ingenuity in employing the routines appropriate to a given background (in this case a Government office) to carry a dramatic purpose relevant to the story. Apart from its technical interest, the scene has interest in showing how Trollope the artist could deal with just that kind of situation which Trollope the man—so honest and so brusque—had often mishandled.

The two friends, Alaric and Harry, have become rivals, competing both for official promotion and for love. In both cases, Alaric has triumphed and his triumph, particularly his triumph in love, has been too much for Harry Norman's affection.

Norman made his appearance at the office on the first Monday of the new year. He had hitherto sat at the same desk with Alaric . . . on his return he found himself opposite to a stranger. Alaric had, of course, been promoted to a room of his own. The Weights and Measures had never been a noisy office ; but now it became more silent than ever. . . . It was known to all that the Damon and Pythias of the

A.T.—7

establishment were Damon and Pythias no longer . . . something dreadful was expected ; and men sat anxious at their desks, fearing the coming evil.

On the Monday the two men did not meet, nor on the Tuesday. On the next morning, Alaric . . . walked into the room where Norman sat with three or four others. It was absolutely necessary that he should make some arrangement with him as to a certain branch of office work ; and though it was competent for him, as the superior, to have sent for Norman as the inferior, he thought it best to abstain from doing so, even though he were thereby obliged to face his enemy, for the first time, in the presence of others.

" Well, Mr. Embryo," said he, speaking to the new junior, and standing with his back to the fire in an easy way, as though there was nothing wrong under the sun, or at least nothing at the Weights and Measures, " Well, Mr. Embryo, how do you get on with those calculations ? "

" Pretty well, I believe sir, . . . "

" Ah ! yes ; that will do very well," said Alaric, taking up one of the sheets and looking at it with an assumed air of great interest. Though he acted his part pretty well, his mind was very far removed from Mr. Embryo's efforts.

Norman sat at his desk, as black as a thunder cloud, with his eyes turned intently at the paper before him. . . .

" By the by, Norman," said Alaric, " when will it suit you to look through those Scotch papers with me ? "

" My name, sir, is Mr. Norman," said Harry, getting up and standing by his chair with all the firmness of a Paladin of old.

" With all my heart," said Alaric. " In speaking to you I can have but one wish, and that is to do so in any way that may best please you."

" Any instructions you may have to give I will attend to, as far as my duty goes," said Norman.

And then, Alaric, pushing Mr. Embryo from his chair without much ceremony, sat down opposite to his former friend, and said and did what he had to say and do with an easy unaffected air, in which there was at any rate, none of the usual superciliousness of a neophyte's authority. Norman was too agitated to speak reasonably, or to listen calmly, but Alaric knew that though he might not do so to-day, he would to-morrow, or if not to-morrow, then the next day ; and so from day to day he came into Norman's room and transacted his business.  Mr. Embryo got accustomed to looking through the window at the Council Office for the ten minutes that he remained there, and Norman also became reconciled to the custom.

# IX

IT is scarcely possible to review or even to assess the work
of a man who wrote so much as Trollope wrote, who
created so large a world, comprehending people of such
variety, and people so completely conceived. So much of
what delights must be left out ; not only because a thorough
analysis of his work would equal his own output in length,
but also because much of his quality—quality which showed
itself variously in pathos, humour, penetration, delicacy
or what one might describe as a sense of human right
feeling—cannot best be apprehended through description ;
it is communicable only from Trollope direct to the
reader.

One can only say that Trollope, besides creating a world
for his readers, also contrives by his writings to give an added
substance to the existing world : he acts as a stereoscope so
that the living world becomes more completely three
dimensional to us after we have read his books. If the title
of artist can be allowed to those who know little about
heaven, but who can give greater substance to earth, then
Trollope earns that title.

To those who love Trollope this is a matter of only
dialectical importance ; it is enough for them that he will
never fail to divert ; to delight with his comedy and acute-
ness, to stimulate with his wisdom and experience and to
open the heart with his tenderness and understanding. His
readers feel a personal and intimate relation with him as
the creator of the novels that differs little from friendship,

and so completely was he " realised " as a writer that there is no compulsive curiosity to investigate into the inner nature of the man, to turn over what, in his candidly reserved Autobiography, he did choose to tell of himself in order to find what might to some analytical eye be hidden from him and from us. Such investigations have, indeed, been sometimes made, but they have added nothing to our knowledge of Trollope—who remains his own best biographer—and nothing to the pleasure or wisdom which his books give.

Nevertheless those who read his Autobiography will find themselves entering into an unusually sympathetic understanding with the man, Anthony Trollope—an understanding which is distinct from the intimacy they may feel with Trollope the artist and creator. Impatient, intolerant, limited in his intellectual apprehensions (and aware of it) he may have been ; but there are the positive qualities which give depth and robustness to a nature—honesty, self-respect, generosity, courage and, above all, zest for living. That militant quality which made him rise at five and work through his stint of novel-writing, which sent him hunting when he was too blind to see the fences, which made him throw down challengingly his common-sense approach to creative work, calls to a comradeship with him sixty years after his death. The noble reserve with which he closes his book, in the passage beginning " It will not, I trust, be supposed by any reader that I have intended in this so-called autobiography to give a record of my inner life " commands a respect which death and fame cannot obliterate. Yet, as though to compensate for what might be taken as a gesture of exclusion, a shutting of the door, he closes this book—the book which he directed to be published only after his death—with his own unforgettable valediction to us :

> Now I stretch out my hand, and from the further shore I bid adieu to all who have cared to read among the many words that I have written.

# BIBLIOGRAPHY

MICHAEL SADLEIR'S *Trollope* lists all Trollope's works and provides sufficient references for any but the most studious researchers. A more complete bibliography of Trollope and Trollopiana is given in *The Trollopes: The Chronicle of a Writing Family* by L. P. and R. P. Stebbins. This also includes some biographical material not found in Mr. Sadleir's book, but as a biography of Anthony Trollope it is recommended with caution since the subject is treated fancifully and with prejudice.

A most useful work is *A Guide to Trollope* by W. G. and J. T. Gerould which lists not only all the novels, but also all Trollope's characters and place names and most of the authoritative works on him—all admirably annotated. It also provides several Barsetshire maps. This book does not, however, include the non-fiction works.

Also, published 1951, there are *The Letters of Anthony Trollope* edited by Bradford Allen Booth. Many of these are extremely interesting for the light they throw on Trollope's character and attitudes; but there is a good deal of trivia which only the most devoted of afficionados will wish to wade through.

It is perhaps hardly necessary to say that social history, memoirs and boigraphies of Trollope's contemporaries are as necessary reading as are the studies of Trollope himself if the reader is trying to get a balanced picture of Trollope as a writer and as a personality.

# INDEX

[Titles of books are printed in capitals : characters in novels are in italics.]